Pots to Knit & Crochet

GINA ALTON

Pots to Knit & Crochet

GUILD OF MASTER CRAFTSMAN PUBLICATIONS

First published 2011 by
Guild of Master Craftsman Publications Ltd
Castle Place, 166 High Street,
Lewes, East Sussex BN7 1XU

Text and designs © Gina Alton, 2011
Copyright in the Work © GMC Publications Ltd, 2011

ISBN 978-1-86108-805-5

Publisher: Jonathan Bailey
Production Manager: Jim Bulley
Managing Editor: Gerrie Purcell
Senior Project Editor: Virginia Brehaut
Managing Art Editor: Gilda Pacitti
Design: Rob Janes
Photographer: Laurel Guilfoyle

Set in Gill Sans

Colour origination by GMC Reprographics
Printed and bound in China by Hing Yip Printing Co. Ltd

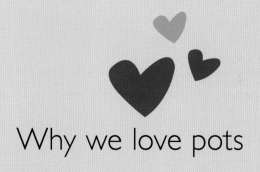

Why we love pots

POTS HAVE been around for thousands of years in countless different styles and materials that represent individual cultures, tradition and (of course) functionality. Today, we still have that innate inspiration to fashion pots that are both attractive and practical – for either everyday or 'special' use. This collection of gorgeous knitted and crocheted pots will hopefully represent the personalities, histories, homes and needs of those who make them.

'Yarn pottery' is a fun and practical modern twist on traditional pot-making. You can make a mini-cottage for your house keys, a piggy bank for your pennies, a box for your beads or even a vase for violets grown in your very own garden. With 30 projects to choose from, there is something for everyone: even pretty pots in which to nest your knitting needles and hooks.

Contents

Dress up your windowsill herbs with this rustic-looking pot. Aran-weight yarn used double produces a chunky-style fabric. Garter stitch against a stocking stitch background forms a simple relief pattern at the centre of each motif.

Terracotta herb pot

Materials

Aran-weight yarn (2 strands used together throughout)
(3 x 50g balls in pure wool were used for this pot)
A pair of 4mm (UK8:US6) needles
Darning needle
Scissors
Potted herb plant (in a leak-proof pot)

Size

Finished measurement is approximately 4in (10cm)
in width, depth and height

Tension

One chart repeat (20 sts and 30 rows) to 4¼in (10.5cm)
in width, measured over pattern on 4mm needles *after blocking*. Before blocking, the fabric is very wavy and of smaller dimensions. However, tension is not critical for this project.

Pattern notes

You may like to press the pieces very lightly, or not at all.
This will produce a quite different effect, with the natural curves of the pattern stitch very much intact. The fabric will be stretchier and quite wavy.

Method

The four sides are made in one long sideways-knitted strip. The base is a single motif knitted separately. These two pieces are steam-pressed and blocked to size. Mattress stitch joins the 'sides' piece into a loop; then the base is stitched on. The pot is then turned inside out and the seams are resewn to gather in the fabric. When turned right-side out again, the garter-stitch seams are more pronounced, giving more of a defined cube shape to the finished pot.

Sides

Use 2 strands tog throughout.
Cast on 20 sts and work either from the text below or foll chart opposite.
Rows 1–3: Knit.
Row 4: K2, p16, k2.
Row 5: Knit.
Row 6: K2, p16, k2.
Row 7: Knit.
Row 8: K2, p16, k2.
Row 9: Knit.
Row 10: K2, p4, k8, p4, k2.
Row 11: Knit.
Row 12: K2, (p4, k2) 3 times.
Row 13: Knit.
Row 14: K2, (p4, k2) 3 times.
Row 15: Knit.
Row 16: K2, (p4, k2) 3 times.
Row 17: Knit.
Row 18: K2, (p4, k2) 3 times.
Row 19: Knit.
Row 20: K2, (p4, k2) 3 times.
Row 21: Knit.
Row 22: K2, p4, k8, p4, k2.
Row 23: Knit.
Row 24: K2, p16, k2.
Row 25: Knit.
Row 26: K2, p16, k2.
Row 27: Knit.
Row 28: K2, p16, k2.
Rows 29–30: Knit.
Rows 31–120: Rep rows 1–30, 3 times.
Cast off loosely.

Base

Work as for sides but cast off loosely after row 30 (1 patt rep).

Finishing

Steam-press all the pieces from the WS: blocking to the measurements given, so that each motif repeat measures approximately 4¼ in (10.5cm) square. Press them very firmly with plenty of steam to really flatten the fabric in order to create the desired effect. Note: If you're working with acrylic rather than natural fibres, you'll need a much lower heat and far less steam. Join the cast-on and cast-off edges of the sides piece with mattress stitch. Next, join the base piece to the sides – also with mattress stitch. You may find that it is easier and that you will get a neater finish by using just one strand for sewing the pieces together.

Finally, turn the pot inside out and restitch each seam, essentially adding a second seam that draws together the fabric and makes the seams more pronounced on the RS. Darn in any loose ends and turn RS out again.

Tip

You may prefer to leave the base off this pot altogether, which will give the terracotta-pot effect without the need for a leak-proof plant pot inside. In this case, you might like to press the fabric more lightly as the base will not be there to add stability to the pot.

Terracotta herb pot chart   *20 sts x 30 rows*

Each square = 1 st and 1 row

 **Stocking stitch (k on RS, p on WS)**

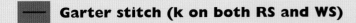 **Garter stitch (k on both RS and WS)**

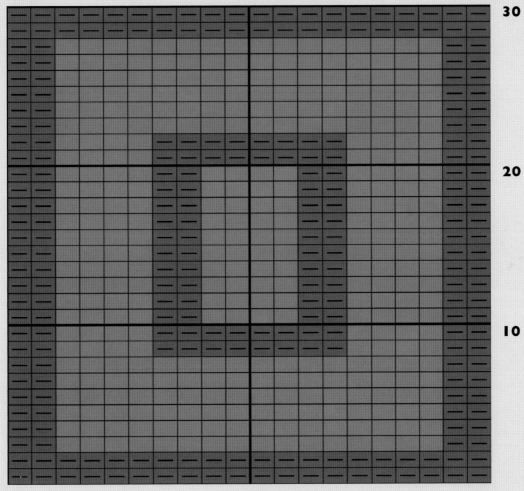

Variegated yarn in a myriad of jewel and earth tones lends depth
and interest to this reversible bowl. The edge can be turned back
for an even finish or turned up for a more bohemian look.

Stripy bowl

Materials

Variegated chunky yarn
(1 x 200g ball in a marble-effect acrylic
    yarn was used for this bowl)
An 8mm (UK0:USL/11) crochet hook
Darning needle and scissors

Size

The finished size of this bowl (including turned-down lip)
is approximately 9½in (24cm).

Tension

Work first 8 rounds of inner bowl piece. The diameter
measurement across the first 7 rounds should measure
roughly 3in (7.5cm). This is a guide only and not critical
to the final result.

POTS TO KNIT & CROCHET

Method

The bowl is worked in crochet throughout, in chunky yarn with an 8mm hook and in amigurumi-style dc spiral rounds. First work the inner bowl. Then make the outer bowl, but do not fasten off. Put the two bowls together (right sides outwards) and continue on to make the edging, working one round dc (working each stitch through both pieces to join) and then a second round of (sk1, ss1) to draw the fabric in.

Inner piece

Mk floop and 1ch.

Round 1: 6dc into floop (6 sts).

Round 2: Dc2inc 6 times (12 sts).

Round 3: (1dc, dc2inc) 6 times (18 sts).

Round 4: (2dc, dc2inc) 6 times (24 sts).

Round 5: (3dc, dc2inc) 6 times (30 sts).

Round 6: (4dc, dc2inc) 6 times (36 sts).

Round 7: (5dc, dc2inc) 6 times (42 sts).

Round 8: (6dc, dc2inc) 6 times (48 sts).

Round 9: (7dc, dc2inc) 6 times (54 sts).

Round 10: (8dc, dc2inc) 6 times (60 sts).

Round 11: (9dc, dc2inc) 6 times (66 sts).

Round 12: (10dc, dc2inc) 6 times (72 sts).

Round 13: (11dc, dc2inc) 6 times (78 sts).

Round 14: (12dc, dc2inc) 6 times (84 sts).

Round 15: Work even in dc.

Round 16: (13dc, dc2inc) 6 times (90 sts).

Round 17: Work even in dc.

Round 18: (14dc, dc2inc) 6 times (96 sts).

Round 19: Work even in dc.

Round 20: (15dc, dc2inc) 6 times (102 sts).

Round 21: Work even in dc.

Round 22: (16dc, dc2inc) 6 times (108 sts).

Round 23: Work even in dc.

Round 24: (17dc, dc2inc) 6 times (114 sts).

Outer piece

Work as for inner piece but do not fasten off.*

Finishing

Place inner bowl inside outer bowl, making sure that the right sides are facing outwards. The outer bowl top edge will be a little lower then that of the inner bowl, but don't worry: this is what will produce the outward-curling 'lip' of the bowl.

Edging

Round 1: Pick up the st loop left from * and work one round in (dc2pcs tog) to end.

Round 2: (Sk 1 st, ss1) to end. This round draws the fabric inwards to stabilize the top of the bowl.

Fasten off.

Tip

Try using a solid colour for the outer bowl and edging to make more of a contrast.

Hide away your cleaning products with this handy basket – there's just enough space for a spray bottle of your favourite cleaner and a cloth. Vary the colour to suit your own taste and home décor.

Clean and tidy

Materials

Tweed DK yarn (3 strands together)
(approximately 250g in dark brown was used for this pot)
A 4mm (UK8:USG/6) crochet hook
A reel of heavy-duty garden wire
Straight metal knitting needle (for shaping corners, optional)
Beadwork pliers
Darning needle and scissors

Size

The size of the finished basket is approximately 4¾in (12cm) in width and depth, and 14in (35cm) in height (including lid and handle). Vary the size by adding or taking away stitches and/or rows.

Tension

Wired crochet is not an exact science. Your own result will depend not only on your crochet tension but also on how loosely or tightly the wire is fed through the crochet stitches and how the pot is moulded to shape.

Method

This pot is worked in spiral rounds through back loops only, with three strands DK yarn used together and a 4mm hook. The basket itself is worked first, from the centre of the base outwards and then upwards towards the top. The lid is worked from the top down in the same way but in a sloping fashion, with the handle worked separately as a 'bobble' and sewn on at the end. Heavy-duty garden wire gives this piece its structure: the crochet stitches are worked around the wire, so the form is produced along with the fabric. See page 151 for more instructions on wired crochet.

Base

Mk wire floop, join yarn and mk 1ch.

Round 1: 8dc into floop (8 sts).
Round 2: (Dc2inc) 8 times (16 sts).
Round 3: (1dc, dc2inc) 8 times (24 sts).
Round 4: (2dc, dc2inc) 8 times (32 sts).
Round 5: (3dc, dc2inc) 8 times (40 sts).
Round 6: (4dc, dc2inc) 8 times (48 sts).
Round 7: (5dc, dc2inc) 8 times (42 sts).
Round 8: (6dc, dc2inc) 8 times (48 sts).

Sides

Rounds 9–41: Work 33 rounds even, shaping the 4 corners manually as you go along.
Ss1 to finish, snip and fold back wire, and fasten off.

Lid

Mk wire floop, join yarn and mk 1ch.

Round 1: 8dc into floop (8 sts).
Round 2: Work even.
Round 3: (Dc2inc) 8 times (16 sts).
Round 4: Work even.
Round 5: (1dc, dc2inc) 8 times (24 sts).
At this point beg to shape the 4 corners (to match base) as you work.
Round 6: Work even.
Round 7: (2dc, dc2inc) 8 times (32 sts).
Round 8: Work even.
Round 9: (3dc, dc2inc) 8 times (40 sts).
Round 10: Work even.
Snip and fold back wire at this point and work rem 2 rounds without wire.
Round 11: (4dc, dc2inc) 8 times (48 sts).
Round 12: Work even.
Ss1 to finish, and fasten off.

Finishing

With knitting needle, shape base and lid corners so that pieces are square rather than round. There are two folded-back wire ends to conceal: one at the top of the basket and the other on the lower edge of the lid. With darning needle and a single strand of yarn, oversew the wire ends stitch by stitch until obscured. Reshape the pot if necessary.

Handle

Mk floop and 1ch.

Round 1: 6dc into floop (6 sts).
Round 2: (Dc2inc) 6 times (12 sts).
Round 3: (1dc, dc2inc) 6 times (18 sts).
Rounds 4–7: Work even in dc.
Round 8: (1dc, dc2tog) 6 times (12 sts).
Fasten off.
Sew handle onto top of lid. Darn in any loose ends.

Tip

Use colours to match the décor of your home. If you don't have any DK yarns (3 strands tog) in the colours of your choice, you could use 4 x 4-ply strands, or 2 strands of Aran or even 1 strand of chunky yarn.

Bangles, friendship bracelets and beaded necklaces can all find a cozy home in this soft mohair-blend bowl. A 100g skein will make several bowls, so why not make a matching set?

Bangle bowl

Materials

Chunky blue-mix variegated yarn
(approximately 30g of a chunky acrylic/mohair
 blend was used for this bowl)
A pair of 5.5mm (UK5:US9) needles
Darning needle and scissors

Size

Will vary depending on tension. Our version measures approximately 3in (7cm) in height and 4in (10cm) diameter.

Tension

Approximately 4 sts and 8 rows to 1in (2.5cm) over garter stitch with 5.5mm needles. Tension is just a guide, as it is not critical for this project.

Finishing

With darning needle, thread yarn through rem 8 sts, pull tight to close and secure with a knot. Sew base seam and side seam. Darn in loose ends.

Method

The bowl is made in one piece, from top to base and in garter-stitch rows. Work even for the sides, then decrease for the base. Sewing up is a single seam along the edges and the ends are easy to darn in and hide.

Bowl

Sides

With 5.5mm needles, cast on 40 sts.
Work even in garter stitch for 20 rows.

Base

Round 1: (K2tog, k8) 4 times (36 sts).
Round 2: (K7, k2tog) 4 times (32 sts).
Round 3: (K2tog, k6) 4 times (28 sts).
Round 4: (K5, k2tog) 4 times (24 sts).
Round 5: (K2tog, k4) 4 times (20 sts).
Round 6: (K3, k2tog) 4 times (16 sts).
Round 7: (K2tog, k2) 4 times (12 sts).
Round 8: (K1, k2tog) 4 times (8 sts).
Break off yarn leaving a tail for sewing and leaving rem sts on needle.

Tip

You could use several strands of DK yarn together in various shades of blue and different fibres for a distinctive effect.

If you are looking for the perfect end-of-year gift for your favourite teacher, why not try making this whimsical parody of the quintessential 'apple for the teacher'? It has its own secret compartment inside too.

Red apple

Materials

Any DK yarn in red
(approximately 50g in a bamboo/cotton blend
   was used for this pot, used double)
Oddments of green and brown DK yarn (also used double)
A 4mm (UK8:USG/6) crochet hook
Small reel of medium-weight garden wire
Beadwork pliers
Darning needle and scissors

Pattern notes

1 strand of Aran yarn could be substituted for 2 strands of DK.

Method

The inner piece (secret compartment) is made first (from bottom to top), worked around wire for the first 12 rounds and then continuing (wireless) to complete the piece like a drawstring bag. A loop is added at the bottom for removing this compartment from the main apple. The outer apple also begins with wirework (worked from top down), then after round 9 continues without wire. A leaf and stem secured to the top of the outer piece act as a handle.

Apple

Cut a length of red yarn approximately 6in (15cm) long: this is to stitch over and conceal the end point of the wire at the end of round 12. Next, wind off about half the red yarn into a second ball, as you will need to be working with 2 strands together. Work in spiral rounds without joins throughout inner and outer apple pieces.

Inner piece

With 2 strands of red yarn, mk wire floop and 1ch.

Round 1: 8dc into floop (8 sts).
Round 2: (Dc2inc) 8 times (16 sts).
Round 3: (1dc, dc2inc) 8 times (24 sts).
Round 4: (2dc, dc2inc) 8 times (32 sts).
Round 5: Work even.

Round 6: (3dc, dc2inc) 8 times (40 sts).
Round 7–12: Work even.
Now snip and fold back wire, and cont using 2 strands yarn only (no wire).
Round 13–14: Work even.
Now use the 6in (15cm) length of yarn and a darning needle to stitch over and conceal the end of the wire after round 12.
Round 15–18: Work even.
Round 19 (eyelet round):
(Ch2 and sk2sts, dc3) to end.
Round 20: Work even, working 2dc into each ch2 sp (40 sts).
Round 21: Work even.
Finish with 1ss and fasten off.

Outer piece

With 2 strands red yarn, mk wire floop and 1ch.
Round 1: 8dc into floop (8 sts).
Round 2–3: Work even (making a narrow tube, with RS facing inwards).
Now working outwards again:
Round 4: (Dc2inc) 8 times (16 sts).
Round 5: (1dc, dc2inc) 8 times (24 sts).
Round 6: Work even.
Round 7: (2dc, dc2inc) 8 times (32 sts).
Round 8: (3dc, dc2inc) 8 times (40 sts).
Round 9: Work even.
Now snip and bend wire, and cont using 2 strands yarn only (no wire).
Round 10–18: Work even.
Round 19: (3dc, dc2tog) 8 times (32 sts).
Finish with 1ss and fasten off.

Stem

With 2 strands brown yarn mk 11 ch.
Row 1: Sk 1 ch, ss10.
Fasten off.

Leaf

With 2 strands green yarn mk 9 ch.
Round 1 (first half) (WS): Sk 1 ch, ss1, dc2, htr3, dc1, ss1 (8 sts so far).
Now rotate piece so you are working along the underside of the ch.
Round 1 (second half) (WS): Ss1, dc1, htr3, dc2, ss1 (16 sts in total).
Now turn piece over to work from the other side.
Round 2 (RS): Ss all around edge, loosely.
Next: Ss along middle of leaf (along original ch, back to starting point).
Break off yarn, leaving a tail for sewing.

Finishing

Inner-piece pull-loop

With 1 strand red yarn mk 1 ch, then mk another 40 ch sts, pulling each one

tightly closed as you go. Break off yarn and thread through bottom of inner piece and knot ends together inside to make a loop. Trim loose ends.

Inner-piece drawstrings (make 2)

With 1 strand red yarn mk 1 ch, then mk another 100 ch sts, pulling each one tightly closed as you go (as for pull-loop, but longer). Break off yarn and thread through eyelets in drawstring fashion, knotting ends to form loops. Sew leaf and stem ends onto top of outer piece. Finally, darn in any loose ends that are left.

Tip
Why not try using a light cream colour for the inner compartment piece, to make it the 'core' of the apple?

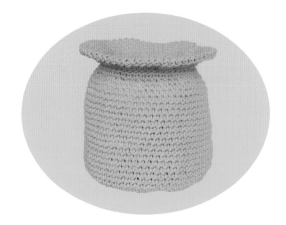

Ordinary parcel string makes an ideal and robust 'yarn' for baskets. It is reasonably malleable, yet the stiffness of the fibre means that the basket is self-standing without the need for a wire infrastructure.

String basket

Materials

12½oz (350g) standard parcel string
(9.5 x 22yd/20m balls, weighing approximately
   1¼oz (34g) each, were used for this basket)
A 7mm (UK2:USK/10.5–L/11) crochet hook
Large-eyed darning needle and scissors

Size

Finished size is approximately 8in (20cm) in both diameter and height

Tension

Approximately 10 sts and 12 rows to 4in (10cm) over double crochet rounds using 7mm crochet hook

Pattern notes

Crocheting with parcel string can be somewhat tough on the hands. Remember to take frequent breaks and not try to rush it.

Method

This basket is worked all in one piece in crochet; from the centre of the base outwards and then upwards for the sides. At the top the work is drawn in through decreases and slip stitches, then outwards again by increasing to form the rim.

Basket

Work in spiral rounds throughout.

Base

Mk floop and 1ch.

Round 1: 9dc into floop (9 sts).

Round 2: (Dc2inc) 9 times (18 sts).

Round 3: (1dc, dc2inc) 9 times (27 sts).

Round 4: (2dc, dc2inc) 9 times (36 sts).

Round 5: (3dc, dc2inc) 9 times (45 sts).

Round 6: (4dc, dc2inc) 9 times (54 sts).

Round 7: (5dc, dc2inc) 9 times (63 sts).

Rounds 8–28: Work even.

Round 29 (dec round): (3dc, dc2tog) 12 times, 3dc (51 sts).

Round 30: Work even in dc.

Rounds 31–32: Work even in ss through back loops on these 2 rounds only.

Round 33 (inc round): (3dc, dc2inc) 12 times, 1dc (63 sts).

Rounds 34–36: Work even in dc.

Round 37 (edging): (Ch1, ss1 into next st) to end.

Fasten off.

Finishing

Darn in any loose ends.

This quirky little pot will add a touch of fun to your home and could easily be made in a range of sizes and colours. The wire crochet construction means that you can shape the twisty top however you like.

Loop-handled pot

Materials

Any DK yarn (3 strands together)
(approximately 50g in a merino/cashmere
    blend yarn was used for this basket)
A 4mm (UK8:USG/6) crochet hook
Approximately 6yd (5.5m) length of heavy-duty garden wire
Beadwork pliers
Darning needle and scissors

Size

The actual size of the basket with lid is approximately 2¾in (7cm) in diameter, and 5in (13cm) in height (not including loopy handle). You can vary the size by adding or subtracting stitches and/or rows.

Tension

Work the first 4 rounds of the base. The measurement across the first 3 rounds will measure approximately 2in (5cm). However, wired crochet is not an exact science. The result will depend not only on your crochet tension but also on how loosely or tightly the wire is fed through the crochet stitches.

POTS TO KNIT & CROCHET

Method

This project is crocheted in spiral rounds throughout, using three strands of DK together and each stitch is worked around heavy-duty garden wire. The basket itself is worked first from the centre of the base outwards, and then upwards to the top. The lid is worked from the top down in a similar fashion but beginning with a loopy handle and then proceeding to form the lid in a cone shape. For further instructions on wired crochet, see page 151.

Base

Work in a spiral around wire.
Mk a wire floop, join yarn and mk 1ch.
Row 1: 8dc into floop (8 sts).
Row 2: (Dc2inc) 8 times (16 sts).
Row 3: (1dc, dc2inc) 8 times (24 sts).
Row 4: (2dc, dc2inc) 8 times (32 sts).
Row 5: (3dc, dc2inc) 8 times (40 sts).
Sides
Rows 6–10: Work these 5 rounds even, shaping sides into the round as you go. Snip and fold back wire, ss2 to finish, then fasten off.

Lid

Work in a spiral around wire throughout.
Handle
Mk a wire floop, join yarn and mk 1ch.
Round 1: 8dc into floop (8 sts).
Next: Work 2dc into the first of the 8dc, then work 18 dc along the wire only. Twist it around as pictured and work 2dc into the 6th of the 18 dc. Work a further 5dc along the wire only.
Lid slope
Round 1: Twist the next bit of wire into a loop, then work 8dc into it (8 sts).
Round 2: (Dc2inc) 8 times (16 sts). Beg to shape the piece into a cone shape from this round onwards.
Round 3: (1dc, dc2inc) 8 times (24 sts).
Round 4: (2dc, dc2inc) 8 times (32 sts).
Round 5: (3dc, dc2inc) 8 times (40 sts).
Round 6: (4dc, dc2inc) 8 times (48 sts).
Round 7: Work these 5 rounds even. Snip and fold back wire, ss2 to finish, then fasten off.

Finishing

There are two folded-back wire ends to conceal: one at the top of the basket and the other at the lower edge of the lid. With darning needle and a single strand of yarn, oversew the wire end stitch by stitch until obscured. Darn in any loose ends, and reshape the pot if necessary.

Tip
Use colours to match the décor of your home. If you don't have DK yarns (3 strands tog) in the colours of your choice, you could use 4 x 4-ply strands, 2 strands of Aran or even 1 strand of chunky yarn.

Just the thing to add a splash of colour to your conservatory or summer house, this hanging basket cover is easy to make and fits the basket like a glove thanks to the stretchy garter stitch.

Hanging basket

Materials

DK yarns in variegated rainbow mix (MC) and yellow (CC)
(Less than 100g in MC and 50g in CC was needed
   for this basket, using budget acrylics)
A pair of 4mm (UK8:US6) needles
Hanging basket 4in (10cm) deep × 6in (15cm) diameter
Darning needle and scissors

Size

Actual measurement of knitted piece 4in (10cm) deep and 5½in (14cm) diameter. Note: Fabric stretches to fit basket.

Tension

Approximately 19 sts and 38 rows to 4in (10cm) over garter stitch with 4mm needles

Method

The fabric is knitted as a single piece in rows, from the top downwards for the sides and then decreasing for the base. The few remaining stitches at the centre base are gathered to close, then the base and side seams are joined. The piece is then simply stretched over the basket like a sock, with no need for fastenings.

Basket

With MC, cast on 70 sts.

Work even in garter stitch for 16 rows.

Still in garter stitch, work as folls:

2 rows CC

2 rows MC

4 rows CC

4 rows MC

6 rows CC

6 rows MC

Base

Use MC throughout

Row 1 (RS): (K5, k2tog) 10 times (60 sts).

Row 2: Knit.

Row 3: (K4, k2tog) 10 times (50 sts).

Row 4: Knit.

Row 5: (K3, k2tog) 10 times (40 sts).

Row 6: Knit.

Row 7: (K2, k2tog) 10 times (30 sts).

Row 8: Knit.

Row 9: (K1, k2tog) 10 times (20 sts).

Row 10: Knit.

Row 11: (K2tog) 10 times (10 sts).

Row 12: Knit.

Row 13: (K2tog) 5 times (5 sts).

Row 14: Knit.

Break off yarn leaving a tail for sewing and leaving rem sts on needle.

Finishing

With darning needle, thread yarn through rem 5 sts, pull tight to close and secure with a knot.

Sew base seam and side seam.

Darn in loose ends.

Tip

You could try varying the stripe sequence for a different effect, or introducing some more colours to the scheme.

The gorgeous reds of this textured yarn transform a recycled bottle into a vase that will show off your favourite cut flowers beautifully. A perfect project for beginner knitters as it uses very basic stitches and only has one seam.

Sunset vase

Materials

Any standard chunky acrylic yarn
(approximately 70g in a marble-effect acrylic
    was used for this vase)
A pair of 4.5mm (UK7:US7) needles
Empty bubble-bath bottle, approximately 8in
    (20cm) circumference × 9in (23cm) height
A handful of pebbles
Darning needle and scissors

Size

Actual measurement of knitted piece is 10in (25cm) in width. Height is adjustable.

Tension

Approximately 5 sts to 1in (2.5cm) over stocking stitch with 4.5mm needles. The knitted vase sleeve fits loosely around the bottle, and you can knit as many rows as you need to obtain the right height; so the tension measurement is not critical.

Pattern notes

If you are new to blocking, try it out on a test piece first. Very short bursts of steam with an iron (on the wool setting) held approximately 6in (15cm) above the knitting work well for the marble yarn used here. The idea is to set the stitches and curb the natural curl at the top and bottom without overdoing it and so making the fabric 'wilted'. You can also use a spray bottle to liberally apply a mist of water to the fabric instead. Ensure that the edges are just a little rolled, spray well and leave to dry completely.

Method

The knitted sleeve is made in easy stocking stitch from bottom to top. 4.5mm needles are used rather than standard 6mm needles (as would normally be recommended for chunky yarn knitting) so that the resulting fabric is dense. The knitted piece is steamed carefully, leaving the cast-on and cast-off edges to still curl a little. The sleeve seam is then sewn up and loose ends sewn in. The bottle (inner vase) is made more stable with a handful of pebbles and the knitted sleeve fits right over it.

Tip

To alter the shape of the finished vase, try weaving in a length of shirring elastic to the wrong side of the knitted sleeve, about 2in (5cm) down from the top to draw the fabric inwards for a 'bottleneck' finish.

Vase sleeve

Cast on 50 sts.

Work in stocking stitch until knitted piece is a little longer than the bottle is tall (making sure to allow for cast-on and cast-off edges to curl a little).

Cast off, and break off yarn leaving a long tail for sewing.

Finishing

Steam the knitted piece very carefully, setting the stitches a little but not overheating the acrylic fibre. Leave the cast-on and cast-off edges to curl over just about ½in (1cm) each, as these serve as borders in their own right. Use mattress stitch to sew the right and left edges of the knitted fabric together into a tube, and then darn in any loose ends. Next, put the handful of pebbles into the bottle to make the base more stable. Run some water into the bottle, add a little flower food and place the knitted sleeve over the bottle. Finally, arrange some long-stemmed cut flowers in the finished vase.

Tip

Adapt the colours of the yarn to suit your décor: seaside blues, sunny yellows, muted greys, pretty pinks or even a striking black and white mix. For this project in particular, it's worth using yarn with a 'touch-me' texture in rich colours that really appeal to you and reflect your personality and the style of your home.

Crocheted mini-baskets use only the simplest crochet techniques. This tiny version is worked in 4-ply yarn with a small hook, but you can easily make bigger ones with the same pattern by using thicker yarn and larger hooks.

Mini crochet basket

Materials

A small amount of 4-ply yarn (approximately 10g in 4-ply cotton yarn was used for this basket)
A 3mm (UK11:USC2–D3) crochet hook
Small darning needle and scissors

Pattern notes

Try substituting other yarns for different-sized baskets: use a 4mm hook with DK, 5mm hook for Aran-weight yarn, 6mm hook with chunky yarn or 7mm hook for super-chunky baskets.

Method

The basket is made all in one piece, from the bottom up. Start with a floop (foundation loop) for a tidy circular beginning and then work in spiral rounds – at first increasing for the base and then working even for the sides. Work a chain for the handle, slip-stitch to the opposite side to secure and then turn and work slip stitch back along the handle. Slip-stitch all around the basket edge once to finish.

Base

Mk floop and 1ch.

Round 1: 6dc into floop (6 sts).

Round 2: (Dc2inc) 6 times (12 sts).

Round 3: (1dc, dc2inc) 6 times (18 sts).

Round 4: (2dc, dc2inc) 6 times (24 sts).

Round 5: (3dc, dc2inc) 6 times (30 sts).

Round 6: Work even.

Round 7: (4dc, dc2inc) 6 times (36 sts).

Rounds 8–11: Work even.

Handle

Now mk 15 ch, sk 18 sts and then work 1 ss (to fix the end of the handle to the other side of basket). Turn and work 15 ss along the handle chain.

Basket edging

Work 1 round in ss all around basket edge (over round 11) to finish.

Tip

Try working more increase rounds, even rounds and handle chain stitches for a bigger basket in the same ply. You could also try embroidering flowers on the basket or sewing on a few tiny flower buttons for decoration.

Finishing

Sew in loose ends on the inside of the basket.

A pot that shows a sense of humour! All your tiny treasures will have their own special place in this cartoon-style red and white toadstool.

Cartoon toadstool

Materials

Any DK yarns in red and white
(approximately 50g each in an acrylic/wool
blend were used for this pot)
A couple of handfuls of budget yarn in red
for stuffing the mushroom top
3mm (UK11:USC/2–D/3) crochet hook
Empty tin can 3in (8cm) high × 2in (5cm) diameter
'Safety' can opener
Darning needle and scissors

Size

The stem on its own is about 3in (8cm) tall and 2in (5cm) in diameter. The size and shape of the top can vary depending on stuffing, but the sample shown is approximately 2in (5cm) high and 4¾in (12cm) in diameter.

Tension

Work first 9 rounds of stem base. The diameter measurement across the first 8 rounds should be roughly 2in (5cm).

Method

The pot is worked in crochet throughout, in DK yarn with a 3mm hook and in amigurumi-style dc spiral rounds. The small hook makes a neat 'close-knit' fabric. The stem is worked first in white, from the outer base upwards and drawing in at the very top. An empty tin can fits inside to provide structure. The top is made then in red from two pieces joined together and stuffed with spare yarn. White polka dots are made and sewn on as a finishing touch.

Stem

With white yarn, mk floop and 1ch.

Round 1: 6dc into floop (6 sts).
Round 2: Dc2inc 6 times (12 sts).
Round 3: (1dc, dc2inc) 6 times (18 sts).
Round 4: (2dc, dc2inc) 6 times (24 sts).
Round 5: (3dc, dc2inc) 6 times (30 sts).
Round 6: (4dc, dc2inc) 6 times (36 sts).
Round 7: (5dc, dc2inc) 6 times (42 sts).
Round 8: (6dc, dc2inc) 6 times (48 sts).
Round 9: (7dc, dc2inc) 6 times (54 sts).
Round 10: (8dc, dc2inc) 6 times (60 sts).
Round 11: Work even in dc.
Round 12: (8dc, dc2tog) 6 times (54 sts).
Round 13: (7dc, dc2tog) 6 times (48 sts).
Rounds 14–32: Work these 19 rounds even in dc.
Round 33: (6dc, dc2tog) 6 times (48 sts).
Round 34: Work even in ss, a bit tightly to draw the fabric inwards.

Lid

Bottom piece

With red yarn, mk floop and 1ch.

Round 1: 6dc into floop (6 sts).
Round 2: Dc2inc 6 times (12 sts).
Round 3: (1dc, dc2inc) 6 times (18 sts).
Round 4: (2dc, dc2inc) 6 times (24 sts).
Round 5: (3dc, dc2inc) 6 times (30 sts).
Round 6: (4dc, dc2inc) 6 times (36 sts).
Round 7: (5dc, dc2inc) 6 times (42 sts).
Round 8: (6dc, dc2inc) 6 times (48 sts).

Round 9: (7dc, dc2inc) 6 times (54 sts).
Round 10: (8dc, dc2inc) 6 times (60 sts).
Round 11: (9dc, dc2inc) 6 times (66 sts).
Round 12: (10dc, dc2inc) 6 times (72 sts).
Round 13: (11dc, dc2inc) 6 times (78 sts).
Round 14: (12dc, dc2inc) 6 times (84 sts).
Break off yarn.

Top piece

With red yarn, mk floop and 1ch.

Round 1: 6dc into floop (6 sts).
Round 2: Dc2inc 6 times (12 sts).
Round 3: (1dc, dc2inc) 6 times (18 sts).
Round 4: (2dc, dc2inc) 6 times (24 sts).
Round 5: Work even in dc.
Round 6: (3dc, dc2inc) 6 times (30 sts).
Round 7: (4dc, dc2inc) 6 times (36 sts).
Round 8: (5dc, dc2inc) 6 times (42 sts).
Round 9: (6dc, dc2inc) 6 times (48 sts).
Round 10: Work even in dc.
Round 11: (7dc, dc2inc) 6 times (54 sts).
Round 12: (8dc, dc2inc) 6 times (60 sts).
Round 13: (9dc, dc2inc) 6 times (66 sts).
Round 14: (10dc, dc2inc) 6 times (72 sts).
Round 15: Work even in dc.
Round 16: (11dc, dc2inc) 6 times (78 sts).
Round 17: (12dc, dc2inc) 6 times (84 sts).

Join top and bottom pieces

Place top and bottom pieces tog with right sides facing outwards.

Next round: With RS of top piece facing you, dc2pcs tog, stuffing with spare yarn just before the end of the round.

Work 4 more rounds even in dc. Fasten off.

Polka dots
(make 14 alike)

Mk floop and 1ch.

Round 1: 6dc into floop (6 sts).

Round 2: Dc2inc 6 times (12 sts). Work 1ss to finish, then fasten off, leaving an end for sewing approximately 4in (10cm) long.

Finishing

Sew polka dots onto top of lid in a scattered fashion using mattress stitch for a neat finish. Darn in any loose ends. Place can inside stem and then the lid on top.

Tip
Use up odds and ends in various bright colours for cheerful mushroom pots in your favourite shades!

Get into the spirit of saving your pennies by creating this little piggy bank. Modelled on the classic shape and style, this savings bank is easy to make using DK yarns and an empty tin can – so making it won't break the bank.

Piggy bank

Materials

DK yarns in budget acrylic (2 strands together)
(approximately 200g in pale pink and approximately 25g
    in hot pink were used, including yarn for stuffing)
Oddments in white and blue
A 5mm (UK6:USH/8) crochet hook
Empty tin can 3½in (9cm) high x 3⅓in (8.5cm) diameter
'Safety' can opener
Darning needle and scissors

Size

Sample shown is approximately 5½in (14cm) tall (including hat) x 7½in (19cm) long (including snout and tail). Size may vary depending on how firmly the body and hat are stuffed.

Tension

Work first 6 rounds of the lining piece. The piece should be about the right size to fit inside the base of the can.

Method

This pot is crocheted with two strands of DK, with the body and hat being made first. Legs, snout, tail and ears are made separately and sewn on: then facial features complete the pot.

Body

Lining

With pale pink yarn (2 strands tog), mk floop and 1ch.

Round 1: 6dc into floop (6 sts).
Round 2: (Dc2inc) to end (12 sts).
Round 3: (1dc, dc2inc) to end (18 sts).
Round 4: (2dc, dc2inc) to end (24 sts).
Round 5: (3dc, dc2inc) to end (30 sts).
Round 6: (4dc, dc2inc) to end (36 sts).
Rounds 7–20: Work these 14 rounds even in dc.
Finish with 2ss, then fasten off.

Outer body

With pale pink yarn (2 strands tog), mk floop and 1ch.

Round 1: 6dc into floop (6 sts).
Round 2: (Dc2inc) to end (12 sts).
Round 3: (1dc, dc2inc) to end (18 sts).
Round 4: (2dc, dc2inc) to end (24 sts).
Round 5: (3dc, dc2inc) to end (30 sts).
Round 6: (4dc, dc2inc) to end (36 sts).
Round 7: Work even in dc.
Round 8: (5dc, dc2inc) to end (42 sts).
Round 9: Work even in dc.
Round 10: (6dc, dc2inc) to end (48 sts).

Round 11: Work even in dc.
Round 12: (7dc, dc2inc) to end (54 sts).
Round 13: Work even in dc.
Round 14: (8dc, dc2inc) to end (60 sts).
Rounds 15–19: Work even in dc.
Round 20: (8dc, dc2tog) to end (54 sts).
Round 21: Work even in dc.
Round 22: (7dc, dc2tog) to end (48 sts).
Round 23: Work even in dc.
Round 24: (6dc, dc2tog) to end (42 sts).
Round 25: Work even in dc.
Round 26: (5dc, dc2tog) to end (36 sts).
Do not fasten off, but just wind off several yards (metres) of the pink yarn (2 strands tog) so you have enough yarn to work the final 3 rounds. Then break off yarn.

Assemble the body

Place the lining inside the can, then put the can inside the outer body piece. Wind off a few large handfuls of pale pink yarn from the 2 balls you are using, and use it to stuff the space between the can and the outer body. It's worth persevering in order to get the stuffing evenly distributed at this point. Use more yarn if need be in order to really stuff it firmly.

Join inner and outer body

Round 27: (Dc2pcs tog) to end.
Round 28: (4dc, dc2tog) to end (30 sts).
Round 29: Work even in ss (a little tightly). This draws the fabric in at the top for a neat opening. Fasten off and sew in end with darning needle.

Hat

First, wind off a small handful of hot pink yarn for stuffing the hat.

Bottom piece

With hot pink yarn (2 strands tog), mk floop and 1ch.

Round 1: 6dc into floop (6 sts).
Round 2: (Dc2inc) to end (12 sts).
Round 3: (1dc, dc2inc) to end (18 sts).
Round 4: (2dc, dc2inc) to end (24 sts).
Round 5: (3dc, dc2inc) to end (30 sts).
Fasten off.

Crown

Round 1: 6dc into floop (6 sts).
Round 2: (Dc2inc) to end (12 sts).
Round 3: (1dc, dc2inc) to end (18 sts).
Round 4: (2dc, dc2inc) to end (24 sts).
Round 5: (3dc, dc2inc) to end (30 sts).
Rounds 6–11: Work even in dc.
Next, put the bottom piece and the crown tog (RSs facing out) for joining.
Round 12: (Dc2pcs tog) until you are nearly at the end of the round, stuff the hat with the handful of hot pink yarn and then (dc2pcs tog) to end.

Shape brim

Round 13: (4dc, dc2inc) to end (36 sts).
Round 14: (5dc, dc2inc) to end (42 sts).
Round 15: (6dc, dc2inc) to end (48 sts).
Round 16: (7dc, dc2inc) to end (54 sts).
Round 17: Work even in ss.
Break off yarn and sew in end.

Legs (make 4 alike)

With pale pink yarn (2 strands tog), mk floop and 1ch. **Note:** Round 5 is worked through *back* loops only but all other rounds are worked through *both* loops of preceding round.

Round 1: 6dc into floop (6 sts).

Round 2: (Dc2inc) 6 times (12 sts).

Round 3: (1dc, dc2inc) 6 times (18 sts).

Round 4: Work even in ss tbl (loosely).

Round 5: Work even in dc through *back* loops, for this round only.

Rounds 6–7: Work even in dc (through *both* loops again).

Round 8: Work even in ss (loosely). Fasten off, leaving a 10in (25cm) tail for sewing. Stuff just a little with pale pink yarn, and sew onto body.

Snout

Work as for legs.

Stuff with pale pink yarn (more firmly stuffed than the legs), and sew into place onto body.

Tail

With pale pink yarn (2 strands tog), mk 35 ch.

Row 1: Sk 1 ch (t-ch), then work 34 ss along ch (34 sts).

Row 2: Mk 1 ch (t-ch), then rotate piece and work 34 ss along underside of chain plus 1 ss into the t-ch from row 1.

Note: On the foll row (row 3) there is no turning chain: just turn and then crochet right into and along the centre of the original chain.

Row 3 (curl row): Wk 1 ss into every second ch st to end (17 sts). The tail will naturally curl into shape with the 'WS' outwards. If it isn't curly enough, you can make a running stitch along the inside to gather it together. Sew onto piggy body and darn in ends.

Ears (make 2 alike)

With pale pink yarn (2 strands tog), mk 6 ch.

Row 1: Sk 1 ch (t-ch), 1dc, 2htr, 2tr (5 sts).

Row 2: Mk 2 ch (t-ch), 2tr, 2htr, 1dc.

Tip of ear: Work (1ss, 1ch, 1ss) into t-ch of row 1, then rotate piece to work along underside of chain.

Row 3: 1dc, 2htr, 2tr.

At this point you have the 5 sts of row 2, 3 sts of the tip of the ear and another 5 sts from row 3 (13 sts).

Next: Work one round along all three sides of the ear, join rnd with a ss and fasten off.

Eyes (both alike)

With white yarn (2 strands tog), mk floop and 1ch.

Round 1: (2dc, 2htr, 3tr, 2htr, 2dc) into floop (11 sts).

Join with ss and fasten off, leaving an end for sewing approx 8in (20cm) long. Stitch on the pupils with darning needle and blue yarn. Secure ends on the WS with a knot and trim short.

Finishing

With darning needle and a single strand of hot pink yarn, embroider the mouth approx ½in (1cm) below snout. Sew in any remaining loose ends. Place hat on top of piggy.

There is something about knowing that there's a new baby on the way that inspires people to pick up those knitting needles and create something special. Here is a straightforward, original design sure to brighten up the nursery.

Baby buds

Materials

DK yarn (2 strands together)
(15g in pink or blue and 10g in white acrylic yarn
    were used for this pot)
A pair of 4mm (UK8:US6) needles
Darning needle and scissors
Cotton-bud container

Size

To fit a standard cotton-bud container, approximately 2½in (6.5cm) in diameter and height.

Tension

9 sts and 18 rows to 2in (5cm) over garter stitch using 4mm needles. Garter stitch is very stretchy so a little variation in tension will be ok.

Pattern notes

Garter-stitch stripe pattern

Rows 1–2: With pink (or blue), knit.

Rows 3–4: With white, knit.

Rep these 4 rows for pattern.

Method

The main piece is knitted sideways in garter stitch, with two rows of pink (or blue) alternating with two rows of white. Stitches are picked up along one side of the main knitted piece and a few rows knitted to form the top hem before being cast off. The base is started in the same way, but we go on to work decreases to draw the fabric in for the centre. Only a single seam is needed to finish the piece.

Tip

Twisting the yarns at each colour change will make a neater edge.

Main piece

This piece is knitted sideways using 2 strands together throughout.

Cast on 12 sts in pink (or blue) and work in stripe pattern (see pattern notes) for 80 rows.

Cast off loosely.

Top hem

Row 1: With RS facing, join in 2 strands pink (or blue) yarn and pick up and knit 44 sts along left-hand side of main piece.

Rows 2–3: Knit.

Next (WS): Cast off k-wise.

Base

Row 1: With RS facing, join in 2 strands pink (or blue) yarn and pick up and knit 44 sts along right-hand side of main piece.

Rows 2–4: Knit.

Row 5: K1, (k1, k2tog) to last st, k1 (30 sts).

Rows 6–8: Knit.

Row 9: K1, (k2tog) to last st, k1 (16 sts). Do not cast off rem sts.

Break off yarn leaving a 12in (30cm) end for sewing.

With darning needle, thread yarn through rem 16 sts, pull tight to close for centre of base and secure with a knot. Thread yarn through those 16 sts again, pull tight to close further, and secure with another knot.

Making up

With darning needle, sew base and side seam. Darn in any loose ends, and place cotton buds container into knitted pot.

Tip

Try a brighter pink or blue for a more striking effect, or double the number of rows per colour change. Alternatively, use a multitude of colours changed at two-row intervals for a rainbow effect – but remember you would have lots of ends to sew in later!

Whether you collect special buttons for those 'someday' projects or just keep odd buttons for last-minute sewing emergencies, this little pot will provide a home for them all. The contrasting trim doubles as a secure fastening.

Button pot

Materials

Any chunky variegated yarn in mixed blues (approximately 80g in a marble-effect acrylic yarn was used for this pot)

Oddment of navy DK (2 strands together)

A 4mm (UK8:USG/6) crochet hook

Empty tin can 4¾in (12cm) high × 3in (8cm) diameter plus lid

6 × white buttons

'Safety' can opener

Darning needle and scissors

Size

The finished pot is approximately 3¼in (8.5cm) diameter × 6¾in (17cm) tall including lid (height may vary depending on amount of stuffing used).

Tension

Work the first 6 rounds of the outer sleeve. The piece should just fit inside the base of the tin can.

Method

The pot is crocheted amigurumi-style in spirals without joins between rounds. The inner sleeve is made first, then the outer sleeve: the can is placed between the two and the pieces joined at the top with a slip-stitch round to close it off. The underneath part of the lid is made first, then the top part of the lid (starting with a 'bobble' handle) and these two pieces are joined with slip stitch. To finish off there is a slip-stitch border in navy, the second round of which incorporates chain-stitch button loops. Six buttons complete the pot.

Pot

Inner sleeve

With chunky yarn, mk floop and 1ch.

Round 1: 6dc into floop (6 sts).

Round 2: (Dc2inc) to end (12 sts).

Round 3: (1dc, dc2inc) to end (18 sts).

Round 4: (2dc, dc2inc) to end (24 sts).

Round 5: (3dc, dc2inc) to end (30 sts).

Round 6: (4dc, dc2inc) to end (36 sts). *

Next: Work even in rounds until sleeve is long enough to reach the top of the can when seated inside. Finish with 2ss, then fasten off.

Outer sleeve

Work as for inner sleeve until *.

Round 7: (5dc, dc2inc) to end (42 sts).

Next: Work even in rounds *one round more* than you did for the inner sleeve.

Next round: (4dc, dc2tog) to end (36 sts).

Join inner and outer sleeves

Place inner sleeve inside can and arrange so it fits neatly inside.

Then place can inside the outer sleeve.

Joining round: (Ss2pcs tog) to end. Fasten off.

Bobble-handle lid

Lid bottom

With chunky yarn, mk floop and 1ch.

Round 1: 6dc into floop (6 sts).
Round 2: (Dc2inc) to end (12 sts).
Round 3: (1dc, dc2inc) to end (18 sts).
Round 4: (2dc, dc2inc) to end (24 sts).
Round 5: (3dc, dc2inc) to end (30 sts).
Round 6: (4dc, dc2inc) to end (36 sts).
Round 7: (5dc, dc2inc) to end (42 sts).
Round 8: (6dc, dc2inc) to end (48 sts).
Finish with 2ss, then fasten off.

Bobble handle

First, wind off about 10in (25cm) chunky yarn for stuffing bobble handle and 60in (150cm) for stuffing upper lid. With chunky yarn, mk floop and 1ch.

Round 1: 6dc into floop (6 sts).
Round 2: (Dc2inc) to end (12 sts).
Round 3: Work even.
Round 4: (Dc2tog) to end (6 sts).
Round 5: Work even.
Use the 10in (25cm) length of yarn to stuff bobble handle.

Note: Bobble handle is now complete. Do not fasten off but rather just continue on from here increasing for the lid top.

Lid top

Round 6: (Dc2inc) to end (12 sts).
Round 7: (1dc, dc2inc) to end (18 sts).
Round 8: (2dc, dc2inc) to end (24 sts).
Round 9: (3dc, dc2inc) to end (30 sts).
Round 10: (4dc, dc2inc) to end (36 sts).
Round 11: (5dc, dc2inc) to end (42 sts).
Round 12: (6dc, dc2inc) to end (48 sts).
Do not fasten off.
Place lid bottom and lid top together (RSs facing outwards).

Round 13a (first half of joining round): (Dc2pcs tog) 7 times, (dc2inc-2pcs tog), 3 times (halfway around) (51 sts).

Next: Place can lid upside down between the lid top and lid bottom. Stuff the top with the 60in (150cm) length of yarn to create a 'dome' effect on the upper lid.

Round 13b (second half of joining round): Now that lid and stuffing are in place, (dc2pcs tog) to end (54 sts). Fasten off chunky yarn.

Edging

Join in 2 strands navy DK.

Round 1: (Ss tbl) to end.
Round 2 (button loop round): ** (9ss tbl), (1ss tbl into next st, work 10 ch pulling each one tight as you go, 1ss tbl into same st), rep from ** to end. 6 button loops.

Finishing

Sew on 6 buttons evenly around pot about ¾in (2cm) down from top edge of pot, so that they correspond to the button loops.
Darn in any loose ends.

Safety first

It is important to ensure that the opened edge of the can is smooth and not sharp. A 'safety' can opener, which bevels the edge automatically, is the ideal tool. If this is not possible, you can apply multiple layers of fabric padding and duct tape around the top edge to ensure a safe non-sharp finish, although this can make the top edge a little bulky.

Tidy away coloured pencils and crayons into this handy bucket. Its cheerful decoration will brighten up the play area and help to inspire some imaginative drawings.

Crayon bucket

Materials

Any Aran yarn in royal blue (approximately 80g in a marble-effect acrylic yarn was used for this pot)

Oddments of DK yarn for embroidered motifs

A 4mm (UK8:USG/6) and a 4.5mm (UK7:US7) crochet hook

Empty tin can approximately 3¾in (9.5cm) high × 3½in (9cm) diameter

'Safety' can opener

Darning needle and scissors

Size

4in (10cm) high (excluding handle) × 3¾in (9.5cm) diameter

Tension

Approximately 5 sts and 5 rows to 1in (2.5cm) over Tunisian simple stitch using a 4.5mm hook. This is a guide only and is not critical to the pattern.

Method

All pieces are worked in 'Tunisian' crochet, which is a combination of knitting and crochet, see page 152 for instructions. The outer pot cover is worked sideways with a 4.5mm hook, and the inner piece just the same but with a 4mm hook. The handle and all decorations are made separately and sewn on.

Bucket

Outer cover

With blue yarn and 4mm hook, mk 28 ch, leaving a long tail at beg. Work 48 rows even in tss, then fasten off.

Base

Foundation row: Pick up 48 loops along side of outer cover and then work second pass of row as usual.

Row 1: (Tss4, tss2tog) to end (40 sts).

Row 2: Work even in tss.

Row 3: (Tss3, tss2tog) to end (32 sts).

Row 4: Work even in tss.

Row 5: (Tss2, tss2tog) to end (24 sts).

Row 6: Work even in tss.

Row 7: (Tss1, tss2tog) to end (16 sts). Break off yarn leaving a long tail, then with darning needle thread yarn through rem sts. Pull tight to close, then secure with a knot.

Inner cover

Work as for the outer cover and base, but with 4mm hook rather than 4.5mm. Place can inside outer pot and inner pot inside can. With darning needle use mattress stitch to sew the top edges of the fabric tog, sealing the can inside. Darn in any loose ends.

Handle

With red yarn and 4mm hook, mk 40 ch, leaving a long tail at beg.

Row 1: Sk 1 ch, then work 39ss along rem ch sts (39 sts).

Row 2: Rotate piece and work 39ss along underside of ch (39 sts x 2). Break off red, leaving a long tail.

Row 3: Turn piece over to work from other side, then (leaving a long tail at beg) in yellow work 39ss along one edge (39 sts in yellow). Break off yellow, leaving a long tail.

Row 4: Leaving a long tail again, join yellow to other side and work 39ss (39 sts x 2 in yellow).

Next, join handle to pot using photos as a guide.

Tree

With dark brown yarn and 4mm hook, mk 15 ch.
Work a tss rectangle over these 15 sts for 5 rows.
Fasten off, leaving a tail for sewing.
Sew on to bucket.

Leaves

Note: Instructions are given here for the 'basic' leaf. Make a couple as such; then try varying the other four by changing the number of stitches here and there.

With green yarn and 4mm hook, mk 6ch.

Row 1: Work even in tss.

Row 2: Work in tss but dec 1 st at each end (4 sts).

Next: Ss counter-clockwise around to beg of ch.

Row 3: Pick up 5 sts along underside of original chain (6 loops now on hook), then work second pass of row as usual.

Row 4: Work in tss but dec 1 st at each end (4 sts).
Ss all around edge of leaf once.
Fasten off leaving a tail for sewing.
Sew the half-dozen leaves on above the tree trunk.

Finally, use darning needle and a small amount of red yarn to embroider a few apples at the top of the tree.

House

Facade

With light blue yarn and 4mm hook, mk 12 ch.

Work a tss rectangle over these 12 sts for 15 rows.

Fasten off, leaving a tail for sewing.

Sew this piece onto the bucket as the facade of the house.

Roof

With orange yarn and 4mm hook, mk 16 ch.

Work 7 rows in total, decreasing 1 st at each edge on second pass of each row (4 sts).

Fasten off, leaving a tail for sewing.

Sew the roof onto the bucket just above the facade.

Door

With navy blue yarn and 4mm hook, mk 8 ch.

Work a tss triangle over these 8 sts for 5 rows.

Fasten off, leaving a tail for sewing.

Stitch on a handle in dark red.

Sew the door to the light blue square.

Window

With light blue yarn and 4mm hook, mk 5 ch.

Work a tss square over these 5 sts for 5 rows.

Fasten off, leaving a tail for sewing.

Sew window onto the right side of the house, and use dark blue yarn to embroider a '+' to indicate individual panes of glass.

Sun

With yellow yarn and 4mm hook, mk 8 ch.

Work 2 rows in total, decreasing 1 st at each edge on second pass of each row (4 sts).

Fasten off.

Now rotate piece and pick up 6 sts along underside of original 8 ch.

Work another 2 rows as before, decreasing 1 st at each edge on second pass of each row (4 sts).

Do not fasten off, but rather work one round of slip stitch all around in order to tidy up the edge.

Now fasten off, leaving a tail for sewing.

Sew the sun onto the bucket and then stitch 'rays' around it.

Cloud

With white yarn and 4mm hook, mk 12 ch.

Work a tss rectangle over these 12 sts for 7 rows.

Fasten off, leaving a tail for sewing.

Sew onto the bucket in a 'scrunched' fashion.

Finishing

Embroider a flower and some grass here and there.

Darn in any loose ends.

Safety first

It is important to ensure that the opened edge of the can is smooth and not sharp. A 'safety' can opener, which bevels the edge automatically, is the ideal tool. If this is not possible, you can apply multiple layers of fabric padding and duct tape around the top edge to ensure a safe non-sharp finish, although this can make the top edge a little bulky.

Real indigo-dyed denim yarn is a joy to use and the fabric will fade like jeans with each wash. Stocking stitch is mixed with both moss and garter stitches, adding textural interest without being complicated.

Denim box trio

Materials

Indigo-dyed denim DK
(1 x 50g ball each in light, medium and
    dark blue were used for these boxes)
A pair of 4mm (UK8:US6) needles
8 stitch markers
Darning needle and scissors

Size

The finished size in denim yarn is approximately 2¾in (7cm) high x 3in (8cm) diameter after washing. There will be some variation in size between different shades of denim yarn as lighter colours 'go further' in your knitting than the darker ones. This can result in a few rows difference in height for the finished bowls.

Tension

With 2 strands of denim yarn, approximately 5 sts and 8 rows to 1in (2.5cm) over stocking stitch using 4mm needles (*after washing*). Tension is given as a guide only and is not crucial.

Denim box trio chart *60 sts x 2 rows*

Each square = 1 st and 1 row

K on RS, p on WS

P on RS, k on WS

| Moss st | St st | Moss st | St st | Moss st | St st | Moss st |

Pattern notes

This project uses 4mm needles – the usual size for DK – but using the yarn double throughout so that resulting fabric is quite close-knit and chunky. If you find this too cumbersome to work with, just switch to a slightly larger set of needles.

Special abbreviations

PM: Place marker (place a stitch marker – or marker thread – at this point, to keep track of where the stitch pattern changes). The stitch marker is simply slipped across with each row worked, maintaining its vertical position throughout.

St st 5: Work the next 5 sts in stocking stitch

Moss st 10: Work the next 10 sts in moss stitch

Method

Each box is knitted in rows from the top downwards in a single piece and using two strands together throughout. Four rows of garter stitch form the top border edge; then for the main pattern four columns of moss stitch (the sides) are separated by sections of stocking stitch (the corners). The work continues as such for the base, decreasing on the last couple of rows to draw the work together at the bottom centre. A side seam and gathering stitch at the base finish off the piece.

Preparation

The first step is to wind off half the yarn into a separate ball, since you'll need to use two strands together. You can either wind off ¾oz (25g), or you wind a new 2-strand ball in a single step, as follows. Reach into the centre of the skein and carefully locate and pull out the end of the yarn. Put this strand together with the other end (from the outer part of the ball) and wind these into a new ball – being careful not to get in a tangle!

Main box piece

Leaving a long end for sewing (at the finishing stage), cast on 60 sts.
Garter stitch hem
Rows 1–3: Knit.
Place stitch markers
Row 4: K5, PM, (k5, PM, k10, PM) 3 times, k5, PM, k5.
Start main pattern
Row 1 (RS): Moss st 5 sts, (st st 5, moss st 10) three times, st st 5, moss st 5. This row sets the pattern sequence. The stitch markers placed on the previous row remind you where the stitch pattern changes occur, and are simply slipped across with each row worked – maintaining their vertical position throughout.
Next: Using chart as a guide, cont in patt sequence until you have just a few metres of yarn left (usually approx 24–27 rows) and ending with a WS row.
Decrease for centre base
Row 1: (K2tog) to end (30 sts).
Row 2: (P2tog) to end (15 sts).
Cast off tightly k-wise.

Finishing

Starting with the long end left before the cast-on, use the darning needle to join the side and base edge seam by picking up the 'heel' of each row's edge-most moss stitch. Secure with a knot, then gather the centre base by drawing the yarn through every second stitch of the cast-off edge. Pull tight to gather and make a knot. Sew in loose ends.

Washing

The final step is to wash the finished boxes. This removes excess dye as well as shrinking the fabric a bit in height. Run them through a full cycle warm wash, then, after spinning, reshape them by hand and leave to dry naturally. The stocking stitch sections form the corners and the moss stitch areas are the sides. For a more 'square' shape, particularly at the bottom of each pot, place a square-based plant pot (or similar item of about the right size) inside while the fabric is drying. You can skip this step if you are using a denim 'look-alike' yarn rather than true indigo-dyed cotton.

Add a homely touch to your office environment with this quick-to-make desk set. An uncomplicated combination of stitches makes this an easy weekend project, ready to decorate your desk on Monday morning.

Desk set

Materials

Any DK yarn (2 strands together)
(80g in a budget acrylic/wool blend was used for this set)
1 pair 5.5mm (UK5:US9) needles
3 × empty tin cans in the following sizes (there is
    sufficient ease and stretch in the fabric to allow some
    variation in the exact size of can used)
    4¾in (12cm) high × 3in (8cm) diameter
    2in (5cm) high × 3½in (9cm) diameter
    3in (8cm) high × 2in (5cm) diameter
'Safety' can opener
Darning needle and scissors

Size

Each finished pot is just a little bigger than the can within.

Tension

Approximately 9 sts and 12 rows to 2 in (5cm) over st st
using 2 strands DK together and 5.5mm needles

Pattern notes

Ridge pattern

Row 1: Knit.

Row 2: Knit.

Row 3: Knit.

Row 4: Purl.

Row 5: Knit.

Row 6: Purl.

Rep these 6 rows for pattern.

Note: The first 2 rows are worked in garter stitch and the following 4 rows in stocking stitch.

Method

The main part of each pot is knitted sideways in a simple 6-row pattern repeat. Stitches are then picked up and knitted along the sides to complete the sleeve and bases. The can structure for each is popped in just before sewing up.

Large pot

Outer sleeve

With 2 strands of yarn, cast on 25 sts. Work 10 patt reps (60 rows). Cast off k-wise.

Inner sleeve

With 2 strands of yarn and RS facing, pick up and k 40 sts along one side of the outer sleeve.

Row 1 (WS): Knit.

Row 2: Knit.

Row 3: Purl.

Rep rows 2–3 until piece measures

approx twice the height of the can (i.e. the width of the outer sleeve plus the length of the inner sleeve), ending with a row 3.

Inner base

Row 1: (K3, k2tog) to end (32 sts).

Row 2: Purl.

Row 3: (K2, k2tog) to end (24 sts).

Row 4: Purl.

Row 5: (K1, k2tog) to end (16 sts).

Row 6: Purl.

Row 7: (K2tog) to end (8 sts).

Break off yarn leaving a 6in (15cm) tail for sewing.

With darning needle, thread yarn through rem sts. Pull tight to close and secure with a knot.

Sew inner base seam.

Outer base

With 2 strands of yarn and RS facing, pick up and k 30 sts along the other side of the outer sleeve.

Row 1 (WS): Knit.

Row 2: (K1, k2tog) to end (20 sts).

Row 3: Purl.

Row 4: (K2tog) to end (10 sts).

Row 5: Purl.

Break off yarn leaving a 12in (30cm) tail for sewing. With darning needle, thread yarn through rem sts. Pull tight to close and secure with a knot.

Sew outer base seam.

Finishing

Place the largest tin can inside the outer sleeve, with the base of it in contact with the fabric's outer base. Tuck the inner sleeve and base gently into the inside of the can, arranging it so that the fabric sits neatly and evenly. Finish by sewing the remaining outer sleeve seam. Darn in any loose ends.

Medium pot

Outer sleeve

With 2 strands of yarn, cast on 15 sts. Work 7 patt reps (42 rows). Cast off k-wise.

Inner sleeve

With 2 strands of yarn and RS facing, pick up and k 28 sts along one side of the outer sleeve.

Row 1 (WS): Knit.
Row 2: Knit.
Row 3: Purl.

Rep rows 2–3 until piece measures approx twice the height of the can (i.e. the width of the outer sleeve plus the length of the inner sleeve), ending with a row 3.

Inner base

Row 1: (K2, k2tog) to end (21 sts).
Row 2: Purl.
Row 3: (K1, k2tog) to end (14 sts).
Row 4: Purl.
Row 5: (K2tog) to end (7 sts).

Break off yarn leaving a 6in (15cm) tail for sewing.

With darning needle, thread yarn through rem sts. Pull tight to close and secure with a knot.

Sew inner base seam.

Outer base

With 2 strands of yarn and RS facing, pick up and k 14 sts along the other side of the outer sleeve.

Row 1 (WS): Knit.
Row 2: (K1, k2tog) to end (7 sts).
Row 3: Purl.

Break off yarn leaving a 10in (25cm) tail for sewing. With darning needle, thread yarn through rem sts. Pull tight to close and secure with a knot.
Sew outer base seam.

Finishing

Finish off as for large pot.

Small pot

Outer sleeve

With 2 strands of yarn, cast on 11 sts.
Work 11 patt reps (66 rows).
Cast off k-wise.

Inner sleeve

With 2 strands of yarn and RS facing, pick up and k 45 sts along one side of the outer sleeve.

Row 1 (WS): Knit.
Row 2: Knit.
Row 3: Purl.

Rep rows 2–3 until piece measures approx twice the height of the can (i.e. the width of the outer sleeve plus the length of the inner sleeve), ending with a row 3.

Inner base

Row 1: (K3, k2tog) to end (36 sts).
Row 2: Purl.
Row 3: (K2, k2tog) to end (27sts).
Row 4: Purl.
Row 5: (K1, k2tog) to end (18 sts).
Row 6: Purl.
Row 7: (K2tog) to end (9 sts).

Break off yarn leaving an 8in (20cm) tail for sewing.

With darning needle, thread yarn through rem sts. Pull tight to close and secure with a knot. Sew inner base seam.

Outer base

With 2 strands of yarn and RS facing, pick up and k 33 sts along the other side of the outer sleeve.

Row 1 (WS): Knit.
Row 2: (K1, k2tog) to end (22 sts).
Row 3: Purl.
Row 4: (K2tog) to end (11 sts).
Row 5: Purl.
Row 6: K1, (k2tog) to end (6 sts).
Row 7: Purl.

Break off yarn leaving a 10in (25cm) tail for sewing.

With darning needle, thread yarn through rem sts. Pull tight to close and secure with a knot.
Sew outer base seam.

Finishing

Finish off as for large pot.

'Home sweet home'... be it a cottage in Cornwall, a bungalow in Brighton, a mansion in Minnesota or an apartment in Arizona. This pot makes an ideal house-warming gift and has space inside for a spare house key.

Welcome home

Materials

Any DK yarns (2 strands together)
(100g each in light and medium brown)
Oddments in dark brown, black and cream
A pair of 4mm (UK8:US6) needles
Empty rectangular tin can and lid with rounded edges
   3½in (9cm) high x 12in (30cm) perimeter
Darning needle and scissors

Tension

Approximately 4.5 sts and 7 rows to 1in (2.5cm) over the stock-rib pattern using 4mm needles and two strands of DK.

Size

The finished pot measures approximately 7¼in (18.5cm) high and 5¼in (13.5cm) wide. This is a guide only: the precise dimensions can vary depending on both sewing-up style and amount of stuffing used.

Pattern notes

Stock-rib pattern (worked over an odd number of sts)
Row 1 (RS): Knit.
Row 2 (WS): (K1, p1) to end.
Rep rows 1–2 for patt. Essentially, RS rows are worked as stocking stitch and WS rows as 1 x 1 rib.

Method

The inner and outer sides (walls) are knitted in a single piece, knitted sideways with two strands of DK together with the can used for structure. The roof is made with various pieces sewn together (the recycled lid enclosed in the fabric) and stuffed to give height at the apex. A chimney acts as the handle for the lid. The front door and two windows are worked separately and sewn on. Yarn is used double for all pieces except the windows.

Walls

The interior and exterior walls are worked in one piece. With light brown yarn (2 strands tog), cast on 40 sts.
Row 1: Work 24 sts as row 1 of stock-rib patt, then knit rem 16 sts.
Row 2: Knit 16 sts, then work rem 24 sts as row 2 of stock-rib patt.
Rep rows 1–2 for a total of 160 rows. The stock-rib section forms the outer wall fabric and the garter stitch part will be the inner wall.
Cast off k-wise.
Fasten off, leaving a long tail for sewing. Use mattress stitch to sew the cast-on edge to the cast-off edge.
Sew the outer base seam, pull the yarn tight as you go to draw the fabric in. Pop the can inside so that the bottom

Tip

As an alternative to the tin-can structure, you could cut out bits of heavy-duty cardboard to size and use strong tape to connect and strengthen the pieces.

rests on the outer base. Reshaping the can a little by pulling the long sides of the can outwards will make it a bit wider for a hand to reach in. If you have done this, then you may need to add some stuffing to level out the outer walls so they look more even. Next, sew the inner base seam in the same fashion as the outer base seam. Tuck in the inner walls and arrange fabric so that it sits neatly inside the can.

Roof
Base (make 2)

With medium brown yarn (2 strands tog), cast on 19 sts.
Work 18 rows in stock-rib patt.
Cast off k-wise.
Fasten off, leaving a long tail for sewing. Make a second piece the same as the first. Put the two pieces tog with right sides facing outwards. With darning needle and mattress stitch, sew along 3 sides, place the lid of the can inside and then sew the fourth side.

Sloped parts (make 2)

The two pieces are made in very much the same fashion as the roof base pieces but are slightly bigger (25 sts and 20 rows).
With medium brown yarn (2 strands tog), cast on 25 sts.
Work 20 rows in stock-rib patt.
Cast off k-wise.
Fasten off, leaving a long tail for sewing. Make a second piece the same as the first. Put the two pieces tog with right sides facing outwards. With darning needle and mattress stitch, sew tog the cast-on edges. Now attach the sloped part of the roof to the base. Using the photos as a guide, stitch them together, leaving an overhang of approximately ¾in (2cm).

Gables

These are the triangular pieces at each end of the A-frame roof.

With medium brown yarn (2 strands tog), cast on 3 sts.

Foundation row: Knit.

Next: Work 14 rows in stock-rib patt, inc 1 st at each end of every second row (17 sts).

Cast off k-wise.

Fasten off, leaving a long tail for sewing. Make a second piece the same as the first. Sew one of the gables in place (see photo for guidance). Stuff the empty space within the roof with medium brown yarn, then sew the second gable on to finish off the roof.

Door (knitted sideways)

With dark brown yarn (2 strands tog), cast on 8 sts.

Rows 1–12: Knit.

Cast off k-wise.

Fasten off, leaving a tail for sewing.

Doorstep

With black yarn (2 strands tog), cast on 9 sts.

Rows 1–8: Knit.

Cast off k-wise.

Fasten off, leaving a long tail for sewing. Sew the cast-on edge to the cast-off edge.

Awning

With medium brown yarn (2 strands tog), cast on 13 sts.

Rows 1–8: Knit.

Cast off k-wise.

Fasten off, leaving a tail for sewing.

Chimney

With dark brown yarn (2 strands tog), cast on 5 sts.

Rows 1–8: Knit.

Cast off k-wise.

Fasten off, leaving a tail for sewing.

Windows
'Glass' backings (make 2)

Make one in each size.

With cream yarn (just one strand), cast on 5[6] sts.

Work 5[6] rows in st st, then cast off k-wise.

Fasten off, leaving a tail for sewing.

Frames

With dark brown yarn (just one strand), pick up and knit with RS facing 5[6] sts along one side of the window backing.

Turn and knit one row.

Turn again and cast off k-wise leaving the last stitch on the needle. Rotate the window right. Now work the second, third and fourth sides as for the first. Fasten off, leaving a tail for sewing.

Finishing

Sew the door to the front of the house and the doorstep just below it. Sew the awning to the front of the house just above the door. Sew the chimney to the apex of the roof.

Keep your make-up brushes and equipment organized in a pot of their own for your dressing table. A small tin can creates the structure and a circle of sponge sheet provides a cushion to protect the tips.

Make-up brush pot

Materials

Any 4-ply yarn (25g in a standard sock wool will suffice)
A set each of 2.5mm (UK13:US1) and 2.75mm (UK12:US2) double-pointed needles
Empty tin can approximately 3in (8cm) high x 2in (5cm) diameter
Small piece of kitchen sponge sheet
1in (2.5cm) length of sticky tape
'Safety' can opener
Darning needle and scissors

Size

Finished size of pot is approximately 3½in (8.5cm) tall x 2in (5cm) diameter

Tension

Approximately 8 sts and 10 rows to 1in (2.5cm) over stocking stitch using 2.75mm needles

Pattern notes

The finished 'sock' has plenty of ease and so fits loosely around the can; so if the can you're using is a slightly different size from the one used here, it should still fit well. Note that each piece begins with two rows of garter stitch. This is because it can be tricky to start off working in the round over three needles when the yarn and needles are very fine. Beginning with a couple of straight rows will help.

Method

The fabric is knitted in two pieces (outer and inner socks), from the top downwards. Both begin with a foundation of two garter stitch rows, after which the knitting is completed in rounds. For the outer sock alone, this is followed by a 2 × 2 rib section. Stocking stitch is used for the main section and base of each, with decreases used to draw the fabric inwards to a close before fastening off. A small piece of ordinary sponge sheet is taped to the inner base of the can to cushion the tips of the brushes. The can is place inside the outer sock and the two pieces joined with mattress stitch. Finally, the inner piece is simply tucked into place to finish off the pot.

Outer sock

* Cast on 60 sts.

Foundation rows:
Knit 2 rows (to create a 'foundation' garter stitch ridge). Now arrange the stitches evenly over 3 needles and beg working in the round. *

Rib section
Rounds 1–10: (K2, p2) to end.

Main section
Rounds 11–40: ** Work these rows in st st (every row knit, since you are working in the round with RS always facing you). **

Dec for base
Round 41: (K8, k2tog) to end (54 sts).
Round 42: (K7, k2tog) to end (48 sts).
Round 43: (K6, k2tog) to end (42 sts).
Round 44: (K5, k2tog) to end (36 sts).
Round 45: (K4, k2tog) to end (30 sts).
Round 46: (K3, k2tog) to end (24 sts).
Round 47: (K2, k2tog) to end (18 sts).
Round 48: (K1, k2tog) to end (12 sts).
Round 49: (K2tog) to end (6 sts).
Break off yarn. Use darning needle to thread end through rem sts, pull tight to close and secure with a knot on WS.

Inner sock

This inner piece begins with the same number of stitches as the outer piece for ease in sewing up; then the stitches are decreased on rounds 2 and 4 so that the fabric fits neatly inside the can rather than being too big.
Work as for outer sock from * to *.
Round 1: Knit.
Round 2: (K8, k2tog) to end (54 sts).
Round 3: Knit.
Round 4: (K7, k2tog) to end (48 sts).
Rounds 5–26: Work as for outer sock from ** to **.
Next: Work as for outer sock from round 43 to end.

Finishing

Cut a small circle of kitchen sponge just big enough to fit inside the base of the can, and secure with a little tape. Ensure that both inner and outer socks are RS out. Place the can into the outer sock; then join both pieces at the cast-on edges using mattress stitch. For a neat seam, ignore the initial garter stitch rows and stitch the 2 × 2 ribbing to the stocking stitch so that the garter stitch edges are hidden on the unseen WS.

A simple one-row puff-stitch pattern is used to create the diagonally striped fabric for this crochet hook holder. Fabulous bamboo yarns are used here, but you can use any colours or fibres to suit your taste, décor and budget.

Crochet hook pot

Materials

Any DK yarns
(1 x 50g ball of bamboo yarn each in medium blue, plum and light blue was used for this pot)
3mm (UK11:USC2–D3) hook
Tin can approximately 4¾in (12cm) high × 3in (8cm) diameter
'Safety' can opener
Darning needle and scissors

Size

To fit a standard tin can approximately 4¾in (12cm) high × 3in (8cm) diameter

Tension

Work first 7 rounds of base. The diameter measurement across the first 6 rounds should be roughly 2in (5cm).
In the puff-stitch fabric, 5 puffs (measured diagonally across the row) measure approximately 2in (5cm). **Note:** The tension is given as a rough guide only and is not critical.

Pattern notes

This project is worked with a finer-than-usual hook for the ply of yarn used, to make a fairly dense fabric – so the silver of the tin can shouldn't be evident through the stitches. Depending on your tension, though, there might be a little bit of show-through with the puff-stitch pattern. To conceal this, you could cut a length of complementary-coloured card to wrap around the can and tape into place prior to sewing on the base piece. Alternatively, make a fabric sleeve and sew into a tube.

Puff-stitch pattern

The puff stitch is formed by working the first half of a treble crochet stitch three times into the same stitch – and then finishing them all off together. Work the first half of a treble (yarn over hook, hook through next stitch, yarn over and pull through stitch, yarn over and pull through two loops). Leave the remaining 2 loops on the hook and work the first half of another treble into the same stitch. Leave these 3 remaining loops on the hook and work the first half of a third treble, again into that same stitch. You now have 4 loops on the hook. Yarn over again and pull through all those 4 loops to finish off the puff stitch.

Method

The main piece is worked first, with every row worked from right to left in a puff stitch pattern. The diagonal effect is made by increasing at the right and decreasing at the left on every row. This creates a parallelogram, which wraps around the tin can and is secured by a diagonal hem. The inner sleeve is worked in a double-crochet spiral from the centre bottom outwards in rounds and then upwards, working three blocks of colour in turn and then increasing for the lip at the top. The outer base is worked separately, also from the centre outwards. Finally, the inner sleeve is joined to the main (side) piece with mattress stitch, the can put in place between the two sleeves and then the outer base sewn on with mattress stitch.

Sides

With plum yarn, mk 30ch.

Row 1: Sk first 3 ch sts and work 1puff in 4th ch from hook, (mk1ch, 1puff in 2nd ch from hook) to last 2 ch sts, sk 1 ch st and work 1tr into the last ch st (13 puffs). Break off yarn. Join light blue yarn to top of 3-ch at beg of previous row (far right).

Row 2: Mk 3ch, work 1puff at base of this 3ch, (mk 1 ch, work 1puff into next 1-ch sp) to end, finishing with 1tr into the tr at the end of the previous row. Break off light blue.

Row 3: In medium blue, work as row 2.

Row 4: In plum, work as row 2.

Row 5: In light blue, work as row 2.

Rows 6–24: Cont in puff stitch and 3-colour stripe sequence as established. Fasten off.

Inner sleeve

Worked in dc spiral throughout (without joins between rounds). With light blue yarn, mk floop and 1ch.

Round 1: 6dc into floop (6 sts).

Round 2: Dc2inc 6 times (12 sts).

Round 3: (1dc, dc2inc) 6 times (18 sts).

Round 4: (2dc, dc2inc) 6 times (24 sts).

Round 5: (3dc, dc2inc) 6 times (30 sts).

Round 6: (4dc, dc2inc) 6 times (36 sts).

Round 7: (5dc, dc2inc) 6 times (42 sts).

Round 8: (6dc, dc2inc) 6 times (48 sts).

Rounds 9–18: Work these 10 rounds even in dc.

* At this point, pop the sleeve into the bottom of the can to check that the circumference is about right for the size of the can, and adjust number of stitches if necessary.

Round 19: Work even in ss (loosely). Break off light blue. Join in plum yarn.

Round 20: Work even in dc, into back loops only.

Rounds 21–29: Work these 9 rounds even in dc.

Round 30: Work even in ss (loosely). Break off plum yarn.

Join in medium blue yarn.

Round 31: Work even in dc, into back loops only.

Rounds 32–36: Work these 5 rounds even in dc.

Note: At this point the sleeve should just reach to the top of the can when placed inside. Work more or fewer rounds if necessary.

Round 37: (1dc, dc2inc) to end (24 incs) (72 sts).

Note: If you have adjusted the number of stitches after round 18 (at the *), adjust number of increases so that you end up with 72 stitches at this point.

Round 38: Work even in dc. Work 2 ss to finish, and break off yarn leaving a long end for sewing.

Safety first

It is important to ensure that the opened edge of the can is smooth and not sharp. A 'safety' can opener, which bevels the edge automatically (as the can is opened), is the ideal tool. If this is not possible, you can apply multiple layers of fabric padding and duct tape around the top edge to ensure a safe non-sharp finish, although this can make the top edge a little bulky.

Base

Worked in dc spiral throughout (without joins between rounds).

With medium blue yarn, mk floop and 1ch.

Round 1: 6dc into floop (6 sts).

Round 2: (Dc2inc) 6 times (12 sts).

Round 3: (1dc, dc2inc) 6 times (18 sts).

Round 4: (2dc, dc2inc) 6 times (24 sts).

Round 5: (3dc, dc2inc) 6 times (30 sts).

Round 6: (4dc, dc2inc) 6 times (36 sts).

Round 7: (5dc, dc2inc) 6 times (42 sts).

Round 8: (6dc, dc2inc) 6 times (48 sts).

Round 9: (1dc, dc2inc) to end (72 sts).

Round 10: Work even in dc.

Work 2 ss to finish, and break off yarn leaving a long end for sewing.

Finishing

There will be a lot of loose ends because of all the colour changes. You need to ensure they are secure (knotted), but as they will be hidden inside, you can just trim them to approximately 2in (5cm) and not sew them all in on the wrong side.

Sew side seam of striped puff stitch piece to make a tube. Use mattress stitch to join top of inner sleeve to side of tubular puff stitch piece. There are 24 puff stitch rows for the main piece, and 72 sts at the top of the inner sleeve: that is, one puff row to 3 stitches as you join the seam. For a neat finish keep to this ratio and stitch along the edge of the puffs rather than the edge trebles.

Place the inner sleeve into the tin can and ease the puff stitch outer piece into place outside it. Use mattress stitch to join the base to the other puff pattern edge. This can be a little tricky as the can is already inside the fabric: work slowly, keep the mattress stitching even and firm and remember the 3-dc to 1-puff ratio.

Tip

A multitude of different looks can be achieved by changing the colours and fibres used in this project. Bamboo or silk yarns provide a wonderful sheen, black and white cotton yarns a made very striking effect and a multitude of colours in mixed fibres gives a 'sampler' effect ideal for using up odds and ends.

Treat your knitting needles to a cozy handmade home in pure and natural undyed wool. The outer sleeve features a sampler-type variety of Aran cabling and the inside provides cushioning for your most treasured needles.

Knitting needle pot

Materials

Any DK yarn

(3 x 50g balls in cream undyed eco-wool were used for this pot)

A pair of 4mm (UK8:US6) needles

2 x empty tin cans approximately 4¾in (12cm) high
    x 3in (8cm) diameter

'Safety' can opener

8in (20cm) length of duct tape

1 x 3in (8cm) diameter circle cut from a kitchen sponge sheet

4in (10cm) x 3yd (3m) cotton crepe bandage (or 2in/5cm x
    6yd/6m masking tape)

Darning needle and scissors

Tension

Finished size is approximately 9½in (24cm) high x 3½in (9cm) diameter

Tension

Approximately 22 sts and 28 rows to 4in (10cm) over stocking stitch using 4mm needles

Method

The structure of the pot is made from two standard tin cans bound together to make a tall tube. The outer sleeve is knitted from the lower edge upwards in various combinations of basic cables separated by columns of reverse stocking stitch. The work is not cast off at this point but continues on for the inner sleeve. The knitted piece is sewn up all along the edge, the inner sleeve is placed into the pot structure and the outer sleeve pulled down over it. The outer base is knitted (from the centre outwards). This piece is then joined with mattress stitch to the lower edge of the outer sleeve.

Main piece

Outer sleeve

Cast on 72 sts.

Foundation row (WS): K1, (k3, p2) twice, (k3, p4), (k3, p6), (k3, p12, k3), (p6, k3), (p4, k3), (p2, k3) twice, k1. This row sets the stitches.

Row 1 (RS): Begin chart.
K1, (p3, k2) twice, (p3, k4), (p3, k6), (p3, k12, p3), (k6, p3), (k4, p3), (k2, p3) twice, K1.

Row 2: Knit the knit stitches, and purl the purl stitches.

Row 3: K1, (p3, T2R) twice, (p3, C4B), (p3, C4B, k2), (p3, C4B, k4, C4F, p3), (k2, C4F, p3), (C4F, p3), (T2L, p3) twice, k1.

Rows 4–6: Knit the knit stitches, and purl the purl stitches.

Row 7: K1, (p3, T2R) twice, (p3, C4B), (p3, k2, C4F), (p3, k2, C4F, C4B, k2, p3), (C4B, k2, p3), (C4F, p3), (T2L, p3) twice, k1.

Row 8: Knit the knit stitches, and purl the purl stitches.

Rows 9–68: Rep rows 1–8.

Inner sleeve

Rows 1–12: K the k sts and p the p sts.

Row 13: Cont as set but work every p3 as a p3tog (52 sts).

Row 14–60: Cont as set (k the k sts and p the p sts).

Inner sleeve base

Row 1: (K2tog) to end (26 sts).

Rows 2–4: Knit.

Row 5: (K2tog) to end (13 sts).

Rows 6–8: Knit.

Row 9: (K2tog) to last 3 sts, k3tog (6 sts).

Rows 10–11: Knit.

Row 12: (K2tog) to end (3 sts).

Cast off, leaving a long end for sewing.

Outer sleeve base

Cast on 8 sts.

Row 1: (Kfb) to end (16 sts).

Row 2: Purl.

Row 3: (K1, kfb) to end (24 sts).

Row 4: Purl.

Row 5: (K2, kfb) to end (32 sts).

Row 6: Purl.

Row 7: (K3, kfb) to end (40 sts).

Row 8: Purl.

Row 9: (K4, kfb) to end (48 sts).

Row 10: Purl.

Row 11: (K5, kfb) to end (56 sts).

Row 12: Purl.

Row 13: (K6, kfb) to end (64 sts).

Row 14: Purl.

Row 15: (K7, kfb) to end (72 sts).

Row 16: Purl.

Cast off loosely leaving a long end for sewing.

Safety first

It is important to ensure that the opened edge of the can is smooth and not sharp. A 'safety' can opener, which bevels the edge automatically is ideal. If this is not possible, you can apply multiple layers of fabric padding and duct tape around the top edge to ensure a safe non-sharp finish, although this can make the top edge a little bulky.

Knitting needle pot chart   *72 sts x 68 rows*
Each square = 1 st and 1 row

K on RS, p on WS

P on RS, k on WS

T2L

T2R

C4F

C4B

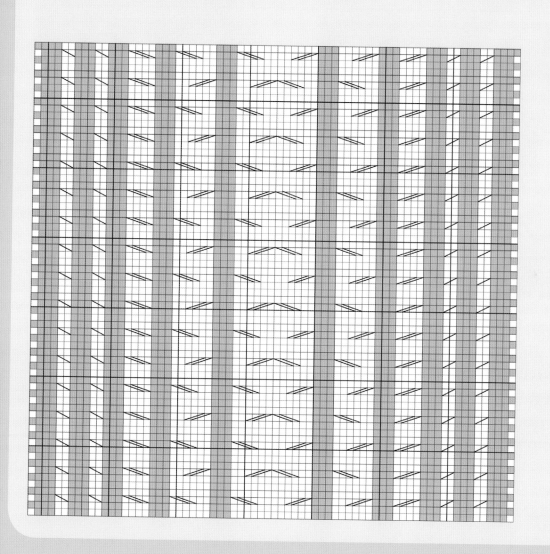

POTS TO KNIT & CROCHET

Making the structure

With a 'safety' can opener, remove both the lid and base of one can, to make a tube. This will be the upper half of the pot's structure. Then remove just the lid of the second can. This will be the lower half of the pot's structure. Join both cans together with some duct tape to make one tall pot. Wrap a length of stretchy cotton crepe bandage around the tall pot and secure the end with a few little stitches using darning needle and a short length of yarn. This ensures that the silver colour of the cans and duct tape do not show through the light-coloured knitted fabric (you can use masking tape instead, if you don't have any crepe bandage). Cut out a small circle from the sponge sheet (a thin circle of foam rubber or even towelling fabric would also suffice) and place it at the base of the pot to serve as a cushion for the tips of the needles.

Finishing

Using the long end left after the inner base is cast off, sew the side seam along the inner base, inner sleeve and outer sleeve. The work now resembles a long tube. Ease the inner sleeve into the pot so that the inner base reaches the bottom and the sides (inner sleeve) conforms to the shape of the pot. You might need to use the blunt end of a knitting needle to even it out.

Now turn the pot upside down and use mattress stitch to join the outer base to the cast-on edge of the outer sleeve. Pull each stitch tightly as you work so that the seam is very firm. Darn in any loose ends.

Tip

The sample was made in a soft pure wool yarn for that traditional Aran-sweater look, but you can substitute any other DK yarn. You could also try varying the cables used in order to create your own unique pot. Just make sure that the fabric is wide enough to fit all the way around the pot, and knit until the piece is long enough to reach the top. Decrease a little as you reach the 'inner sleeve' portion so that the inside fabric is not too bulky.

This stylish pot is really quick and easy to make, is a handy place to put your pennies at the end of the day – and is cheap to make since you can use any old yarns you happen to have on hand.

Penny pot

Materials
25g of super-chunky yarn (OR multiple strands of DK
   used together for the thickness of super-chunky)
A pair of 5.5mm (UK5:US9) needles
Darning needle and scissors

Size
The finished pot is approximately 4½in (11.5cm)
wide x 2½in (6.5cm) wide x 2½in (6.5cm) deep.

Tension
Approximately 4.5 sts and 8 rows over garter stitch,
using 5.5mm needles.

POTS TO KNIT & CROCHET

Method

The pot is knitted in two very similar pieces, from the top downwards. There is a reverse stocking stitch rolled hem, a stocking stitch band, a garter stitch section and finally 2 × 2 rib. Each piece is cast off knitwise and the two pieces sewn together. Smaller-than-usual needles make a firm fabric from the super-chunky yarn.

Side 1

Cast on 20 sts.

Row 1 (RS): Purl.

Row 2 (WS): Knit.

Row 3: Purl.

Rows 1–3 form reverse stocking stitch top edging.

Row 4 (WS): Purl.

Row 5 (RS): Knit.

Row 6: Purl.

Rows 4–6 form stocking stitch.

Rows 7–10: Knit.

These 4 rows form garter stitch. *

Row 11: K1, (k2, p2) to last 3 sts, k2, k1.

Row 12: K1, (p2, k2) to last 3 sts, p2, k1.

Rows 13–20: Rep rows 11–12.

Rows 11–20 form 2 × 2 rib with 1 moss stitch at each edge for selvedge. Cast off k-wise, leaving a long end for sewing.

Side 2

Work as for side 1 to *.

Row 11: K1, (p2, k2) to last 3 sts, p2, k1.

Row 12: K1, (k2, p2) to last 3 sts, k2, k1.

Rows 13–20: Rep rows 11–12.

Rows 11–20 form 2 × 2 rib with 1 moss stitch at each edge for selvedge.

Note: The reason the two sides differ a bit in this section is so that, when sewn up, the 2 × 2 rib joins are tidy at the edges.

Cast off k-wise, leaving a long tail for sewing.

Finishing

With darning needle, use mattress stitch to sew side seams, then the base. Darn in any loose ends.

Tip

You can use any yarns you like for this pot. Use about 4 strands of DK together to make up the thickness of a quick-knit super-chunky yarn, or downsize your needles and use fewer strands for a smaller pot. It is better to use a smaller-than-normal needle size for whatever thickness of yarn you use, as this makes a firm fabric for a self-standing pot.

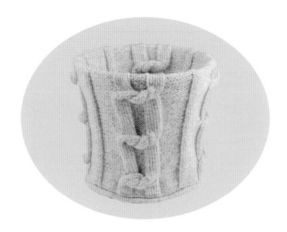

Add a homey touch to your office space with this knotted-cable wastepaper basket. The fabric is easily removed for washing and the structure over which it rests is an ordinary plant pot.

Wastepaper basket

Materials

Any standard Aran yarn

(1 x 400g ball will suffice if using a typical 75% acrylic 25% wool yarn but you may need to allow for more if using a higher percentage of natural fibres)

A pair of 4.5mm (UK7:US7) needles

A 3.5mm (UK9–10:US4) circular needle

1 plastic plant pot approximately 10in (25cm) height x 10in (25cm) diameter

3 safety pins (or stitch holders)

Darning needle and scissors

Size

Finished size is 10in (25cm) height x 10in (25cm) diameter

Tension

Approximately 28 rows to 4in (10cm) over reverse stocking stitch using 4.5mm needles. Cabled fabric is very stretchy width-wise, so that is why only row tension is relevant here.

Special abbreviations

Crossed-k2tog tbl

Sl1, sl next st onto safety pin and hold to front of work, place first slipped st back onto LH needle, move st on safety pin to LH needle too, then k2tog tbl.

Pattern notes

Twisted stocking stitch

Knit through the back loop on RS rows, and purl through the back loop on WS rows.

Column pattern

Row 1 (RS): K3tbl, p10, k7tbl, p7, k7tbl, p10, k3tbl.

Row 2: P3tbl, k10, p7tbl, k7, p7tbl, k10, p3tbl.

Rep rows 1–2 for patt.

Method

The structure of this wastepaper basket is provided by a plastic plant pot. Four identical panels are knitted and then mattress-stitched together to form a long tube closed at one end. The fabric fits right over the plant pot with the cast-on edge at the outer base and the closed end on the inside. The fabric is removable for washing.

The unusual cabling feature is created by working an extra 15 rows for each of the 7-stitch sections and then actually tying these in a knot, rather than crossing stitches as for conventional cables. Additionally, the stocking stitches are 'twisted' by working into the back loops, while the reverse stocking stitch areas are worked in the standard way.

Panels (make 4 alike)

First, wind off a ball of yarn to use for the knot sections.
With 4.5mm needles cast on 47 sts.
Work 10 rows in column patt.
**Knot section begins
Slip the first 13 sts to the RH needle.
Join in secondary ball of yarn at this point and work 15 rows in twisted st st over the next 7 stitches only. Break off yarn and place these 7 sts onto a safety pin.

Slip the foll 7 sts onto another safety pin. Rep * to *.
Note: At this point there are 13 sts left on the LH needle, 3 safety pins with 7 sts each and 13 sts on the RH needle.
Next: Tie the two 15-row twisted st st strips into a simple knot. The first one you knitted is now on the left, and the second on the right.
Take the 7 sts from the twisted st st piece on the left off their safety pin and place them on the LH needle. Next, do the same with the middle 7 sts (the rev st st centre sts), then the 7 sts from the other twisted st st strip and finally move the rem 13 sts from the RH needle to the LH needle.
The first knot is tied and all the stitches are now in place in their new order on the LH needle ready to return to the column patt.
Knot section complete
Work a further 22 rows in column patt. Rep from ** three times. Total of 4 knots.
Dec for inner base
Row 1: K2 tbl, (k2tog tbl), work to last 4 sts, (crossed-k2tog tbl), k2tbl.
Row 2: Work even in patt.
Repeat rows 1–2 to cont decreasing for base until only 2 sts rem.
K2tog, then fasten off leaving a long end for sewing.

Finishing

Sew all four seams using mattress stitch.

Hem

With circular needle and RS facing, pick up and k 180 sts all around the cast-on edge of the joined four panels: 45 sts per panel. Work even in st st for 10 rnds, then cast off k-wise.
Break off yarn.

Hem detail

Join in yarn again at cast-on edge and pick up and k 180 sts again from the RS. Work a cast-off round loosely and fasten off.

Darn in any loose ends.
Turn WS outwards and place base into plant pot (so that the RS is visible inside). Fold over so that rest of the fabric hugs the pot on the outside, and arrange evenly.

Say goodbye to boring pencil pots! Decorate your desk instead with this cartoon-style vase and oversized daisy pencil toppers, sure to brighten your working day.

Pen and pencil pot

Materials

Approximately 100g cotton DK yarn in blue

2 large handfuls of budget yarn in blue for stuffing

Approximately 25g DK yarns each in yellow, white and green

A 4mm (UK8:USG/6) crochet hook (for vase)

A 3mm (UK11:USC/2–D/3) crochet hook (for flowers)

3 x pencils or pens

Empty tin can approximately 4¾in (12cm) high x
    3in (8cm) diameter

'Safety' can opener

Darning needle and scissors

Size

Approximate size of finished vase is 5in (12.5cm) high x 14in (35cm) circumference

Tension

Work first 7 rounds of inner base, then work even for 6 rounds. The piece should fit comfortably inside the can without being too bulky. Use a larger or smaller hook if necessary.

Pattern notes

The stitched white spiral on the pencil pot could be worked prior to placing the can into the outer sleeve for stuffing and joining, but take care not to pull the stitches too tight as the blue fabric needs to retain its elasticity so the stuffing is able to fill out the curvy 'vase' shape.

Method

Both the inner and outer sleeve of the pot are worked in spiral rounds throughout. The inner piece is worked first, from the centre of the base outwards and then upwards for the sides. The outer sleeve begins in the same fashion, albeit with an extra round of increases at the base in order to fit around the outside of the can. Increase rounds begin the shaping for the vase, then decrease rounds bring the fabric in again at the neck of the vase. The inner sleeve is placed inside the can, then the can is put inside the outer sleeve and handfuls of yarn used to fill the convex middle area of the outer vase. The inner and outer sleeves are now joined by double crocheting the two pieces together. Further increase rounds result in the frill at the top. To finish, stitches in white are worked in a loose spiral for decoration. The yellow flower centre is worked as two pieces (front and back) joined together and stuffed with a little matching yarn. White is joined in, a row of slip stitch work to transition to the new colour and then the petals worked over two rounds.

Pencil pot

Both inner and outer pieces are worked in dc spiral throughout (without joins between rounds).

Inner sleeve base

With 4mm hook and blue yarn, mk floop and 1ch.
Round 1: 6dc into floop (6 sts).
Round 2: (Dc2inc) 6 times (12 sts).
Round 3: (1dc, dc2inc) 6 times (18 sts).
Round 4: (2dc, dc2inc) 6 times (24 sts).
Round 5: (3dc, dc2inc) 6 times (30 sts).
Round 6: (4dc, dc2inc) 6 times (36 sts).
Round 7: (5dc, dc2inc) 6 times (42 sts).

Inner sleeve sides

Work even in dc rounds until piece is long enough to reach about 1in (2.5cm) above top of can when sleeve is placed inside.
2ss to finish, then fasten off.

Outer sleeve base

With 4mm hook and blue yarn, mk floop and 1ch.
Round 1: 6dc into floop (6 sts).
Round 2: (Dc2inc) 6 times (12 sts).
Round 3: (1dc, dc2inc) 6 times (18 sts).
Round 4: (2dc, dc2inc) 6 times (24 sts).
Round 5: (3dc, dc2inc) 6 times (30 sts).
Round 6: (4dc, dc2inc) 6 times (36 sts).
Round 7: (5dc, dc2inc) 6 times (42 sts).
Round 8: (6dc, dc2inc) 6 times (48 sts).

Outer sleeve sides

Rounds 9–14: Work even in dc.
Round 15: (7dc, dc2inc) to end (54 sts).
Round 16: (8dc, dc2inc) to end (60 sts).
Round 17: Work even in dc.
Round 18: (9dc, dc2inc) to end (66 sts).
Round 19: (10dc, dc2inc) to end (72 sts).
Rounds 20–25: Work even in dc.
Round 26: (10dc, dc2tog) to end (66 sts).
Round 27: (9dc, dc2tog) to end (60 sts).
Rounds 28–29: Work even in dc.
Round 30: (8dc, dc2tog) to end (54 sts).
Round 31: (7dc, dc2tog) to end (48 sts).

Round 32: Work even in dc.
Round 33: (6dc, dc2tog) to end (42 sts).
Rounds 34–35: Work even in dc.
Do not fasten off yarn.

Fitting inner and outer sleeves to pot

Turn inner sleeve inside out (WS facing outwards, so that the right side is seen from the inside) and ease it into the can so that the base reaches the bottom and the sides conform to the contours of the can. Next, place the tin can inside the outer sleeve and stuff the middle section as evenly as possible. This might take a little time to achieve, and you may find that cutting the handfuls of yarn into shorter lengths can make it easier to distribute the stuffing yarn evenly.

Join inner and outer sleeves

Pick up the loop left after the end of round 35 which was not fastened off.
Round 1: Dc the two pieces tog by working each dc of this round into both the next stitch from the outer sleeve and the corresponding stitch from the inner sleeve (42 sts).
Round 2: (2dc, dc2inc) to end (56 sts).
Round 3: (3dc, dc2inc) to end (70 sts).
Round 4: (4dc, dc2inc) to end (84 sts).
Work 2dc, then 2ss to finish.
Fasten off.

Contrast stitching

With darning needle and a long length of white yarn, work a spiral of running stitches around the vase along every third row until you have about eight rounds of white. Now work a second layer of stitching by working around each 'float' of the first spiral. Where you need to join in a new length of yarn, just knot the end of one piece to the beginning of another and use the darning needle to pull the ends through to the inside of the fabric/stuffing.

Daisy pencil toppers

Either make three alike, or make each daisy unique by experimenting with stitch numbers and types (see tip box). Before starting, wind off about 8in (20cm) of yellow yarn to use for stuffing the centre later.

Flower centre (front)

Work throughout in dc rounds with no joins between rounds.
With 3mm hook and yellow yarn, mk floop and 1ch.
Round 1: 6dc into floop (6 sts).
Round 2: (Dc2inc) 6 times (12 sts).
Rounds 3–4: Work even in dc.
Work 2ss to finish, then fasten off.

Joining flower centres (back and front)

Work one round of slip stitch all around, working into the next stitch of the back as well as the corresponding stitch of the front with every ss, stuffing with the length of yarn wound off earlier just before closing (14 sts).
Fasten off.

Petals

Round 1: With 3mm hook and with flower centre front facing you, join white yarn with a slip stitch and work one round loosely into the joining round just worked in yellow (14 sts).

Round 2: * Work 1ss into next st, mk 8ch, (sk 1 ch, 1dc into each of the rem 7 ch sts), then 1ss into st at base of the 8ch. Rep from * to end (14 petals half-finished).

Round 3: Now turn work so that the WS is facing you. * Work 1ss into each st up along side of petal, 1ss into turning ch, then 1ss into each st down along other side of petal. Rep from * to end (14 petals now completed). **Note:** If you find that some of the yellow is showing through from the back of the petal bases, just do a little running stitch around in white to tidy it up.

Stem

Work throughout in dc rounds with no joins between rounds. With 3mm hook and blue yarn, mk floop and 1ch.

Round 1: 7dc into floop (7 sts).

Round 2–19: Work even in dc. Work 2ss to finish, then fasten off.

Join flower to stem

With darning needle and a length of yellow yarn, firmly stitch flower centre to tip of stem.

Finishing

Darn in any loose ends. Place daisy flower toppers onto pencils (or pens) and arrange in the vase.

Tip

You can make each flower unique, not just by substituting other colours and fibres but also by making subtle changes to the pattern details. Try working more or fewer stitches into the foundation round of the flower centre, adjusting the length of the petals by working a different number of chain stitches on round 2, or working combinations of double crochet and half treble crochet around round 3.

This stylish dish comes complete with pebbles. The three larger pebbles are actually little pots with wooden toggle closures – perfect for hiding away a spare key, tiny treasure or even a secret love note to that special someone.

Pebble dish

Materials

1 x 100g ball white dishcloth cotton DK yarn

10 small balls of 'pebble'-coloured yarn in various
    fibres and plies of your choice

A 3mm (UK11:USC/2–D/3) crochet hook

3 x small wooden toggles

Darning needle and scissors

Size

The finished size of the dish is 8in (20cm) across x approximately 2in (5cm) at corners (edges curve up gently)

Tension

Work the first 6 rounds of the base. The measurement of the diameter of the first 5 rounds should be approximately 2in (5cm). The tension information is given as a guide only and some variation in tension will not adversely affect the result.

Pattern notes

Both the dish and the pebbles are worked in dc spirals, with no joins between rounds. The dish, however, is worked through back loops only whereas the pebbles are worked through both loops.

Method

The dish is worked first in DK and spiral crochet rounds through back loops only – with four 'dc3incs' per round to create corners and subtle upwards shaping. The pebbles are worked in a variety of fibres and muted colours: use any yarns that appeal to you. The smaller pebbles are stuffed and closed, whereas the larger three feature openings with toggle closures and so are mini-pots in their own right. Each pebble is worked in spiral rounds with its own series of increases and decreases for shaping.

Dish

Work through back loops only, throughout.

Bottom layer

With white cotton yarn, mk floop and 1ch.

Round 1: 8dc into floop (8 sts).
Round 2: (1dc, dc3inc) 4 times (16 sts).
Round 3: 1dc, (dc3inc, dc3) 3 times, dc3inc, dc2 (24 sts).
Round 4: 2dc, (dc3inc, dc5) 3 times, dc3inc, dc3 (32 sts).
Round 5: 3dc, (dc3inc, dc7) 3 times, dc3inc, dc4 (40 sts).
Round 6: 4dc, (dc3inc, dc9) 3 times, dc3inc, dc5 (48 sts).
Round 7: 5dc, (dc3inc, dc11) 3 times, dc3inc, dc6 (56 sts).
Round 8: 6dc, (dc3inc, dc13) 3 times, dc3inc, dc7 (64 sts).
Round 9: 7dc, (dc3inc, dc15) 3 times, dc3inc, dc8 (72 sts).
Round 10: 8dc, (dc3inc, dc17) 3 times, dc3inc, dc9 (80 sts).
Round 11: 9dc, (dc3inc, dc19) 3 times, dc3inc, dc10 (88 sts).
Round 12: 10dc, (dc3inc, dc21) 3 times, dc3inc, dc11 (96 sts).
Round 13: 11dc, (dc3inc, dc23) 3 times, dc3inc, dc12 (104 sts).
Round 14: 12dc, (dc3inc, dc25) 3 times, dc3inc, dc13 (112 sts).
Round 15: 13dc, (dc3inc, dc27) 3 times, dc3inc, dc14 (120 sts).

Tip

A finer than usual hook is used for the dish to create a firm fabric. If you find this too fiddly, change to a 3.5mm or even 4mm hook – but be aware that that this will require more yarn unless you work fewer rounds to compensate. The pebbles are worked in the same small 3mm hook, but would work equally well with a 3.25mm or 3.5mm hook.

Round 16: 14dc, (dc3inc, dc29) 3 times, dc3inc, dc15 (128 sts).
Round 17: 15dc, (dc3inc, dc31) 3 times, dc3inc, dc16 (136 sts).
Round 18: 16dc, (dc3inc, dc33) 3 times, dc3inc, dc17 (144 sts).
Round 19: 17dc, (dc3inc, dc35) 3 times, dc3inc, dc18 (152 sts).
Round 20: 18dc, (dc3inc, dc37) 3 times, dc3inc, dc19 (160 sts).
Work 2ss to finish, then fasten off.

Top layer

Work as for first layer but do not fasten off.

Joining the two layers

Put the two layers together with right sides facing outwards. Work a joining round by slip-stitching through both layers with each stitch and taking care to match up the corner increases so that the pieces fit together properly. Break off yarn.

Pebbles

Round pebbles (make an assortment in various colours)

First, unravel a 2yd (2m) length of yarn and set aside for stuffing the pebble. Mk floop and 1ch.

Round 1: 6dc into floop (6 sts).
Round 2: (Dc2inc) 6 times (12 sts).
Round 3: (1dc, dc2inc) 6 times (18 sts).
Round 4: Work even in dc.
Round 5: (2dc, dc2inc) 6 times (24 sts).
Rounds 6–7: Work even in dc.
Round 8: (2dc, dc2tog) 6 times (18 sts).
Rounds 9–10: Work even in dc.
Round 11: (1dc, dc2tog) 6 times (12 sts).
Round 12: (Dc2tog) 6 times (6 sts).
Break off yarn leaving an end for sewing approx 6in (15cm) long. Thread the darning needle with that end, weave through tops of rem sts, pull tight to close and secure with a knot. Tuck loose end into pebble.

Oval pebble pots (make 3, in various colours)

Mk floop and 1ch.

Round 1: 6dc into floop (6 sts).
Round 2: (Dc2inc) 6 times (12 sts).
Round 3: (1dc, dc2inc) 6 times (18 sts).
Round 4: Work even in dc.
Round 5: (2dc, dc2inc) 6 times (24 sts).
Rounds 6–9: Work even in dc.
Round 10 (toggle loop round):
Dc4, mk 7ch (for toggle loop), 1dc into each of rem 16 dc sts (24dc total, plus a 7-st chain loop).
Round 11: Dc4, leave 7-ch loop unworked (just skip it altogether and leave at front of work), 15dc, 1ss.
Round 12 (pot-hole round): (Mk 8 ch and sk next 8 dc sts), 1ss into foll sts, then 1dc into each of rem 15 sts.
Round 13: Work 1dc into each of the 8 ch sts, then 1dc into each st to end (24 dc sts).
Round 14: Work even in dc.
Round 15: (2dc, dc2tg) 6 times (18 sts).

Round 16: Work even in dc.
Round 17: (1dc, dc2tg) 6 times (12 sts).
Round 18: (Dc2tg) 6 times (6 sts).
Break off yarn leaving an end for sewing approx 6in (15cm) long. Thread the darning needle with that end, weave through tops of rem sts, pull tight to close and secure with a knot.

Finishing

Sew one toggle each onto the three pebble pots. Alternatively, use flat buttons in colours to match in order to better disguise the pots. Darn in any loose ends and arrange pebbles over dish.

> ## Tip
> You could try using black for the dish and changing the pebbles to white, or make the dish in cream and use a rainbow of colours for the pebbles. The pebbles could all be similar sizes, or you could make other pebble shapes by increasing and decreasing at random intervals.

Add a splash of colour to any room with this cheerful bud vase. Long-lasting artificial buds are complemented by a bespoke knitted vase jacket – a recycled hand soap container provides the practical underlying structure.

Bud vase

Materials

Any chunky yarn (approximately 25g of a marbled
    chunky acrylic was used for this pot)
A pair of 4mm (UK8:US6) needles
An empty hand soap container (with pump dispenser
    removed) approximately 4½in (11.5cm) high × 9in
    (23cm) circumference at highest/deepest point
2 large handfuls pearl barley or dried beans
12in (30cm) length of duct tape
Darning needle and scissors

Size

The finished knitted jacket (with structure in situ) measures approximately 6in (15cm) high × 10½in (27cm) circumference.

Tension

Approximately 5 sts and 7 rows to 1in (2.5cm) over st st using 4mm needles and a typical chunky yarn.

POTS TO KNIT & CROCHET

Pattern notes

If you'd prefer to use freshly-cut flowers, swap the pearl barley (or beans) for a handful of small pebbles, some water and a splash of plant food.

Method

The hand soap container is weighted down with dried grains or beans. The knitted jacket is made all in one piece, from the top downwards. A rolled hem makes a neat edging, the 2 x 2 rib provides a 'polo-neck' and the main part is knitted in straightforward stocking stitch with just a bit of shaping for the base at the end before working a few rows in waste yarn and then casting off. Finishing off is very quick and easy: the sides are joined with a mattress stitch seam, forming a tube shape. This seam will be at the centre back. To avoid having a seam along the middle of the base, the stitches are grafted and the waste yarn then removed.

Vase structure

Rinse the hand soap pot and then leave to dry completely. Pour the pearl barley or dried beans into the pot. Insert the artificial flowers and use the length of duct tape to secure them into place (if necessary).

Knitted jacket

With chunky yarn, cast on 50 sts.

Rolled hem

Rows 1–4: Beginning with a knit row, work these four rows in stocking stitch.

'Polo-neck'

Row 5: K1, (k2, p2) to last st, k1.
Row 6: K1, (p2, k2) to last st, k1.
Rows 7–14: Rep rows 5–6 four times (total of 10 rows in 2 x 2 rib with 1 moss stitch at each edge).

Body

Row 15 (RS): Knit.
Row 16: K1, purl to last stitch, k1.
These two rows form stocking stitch with 1 moss stitch at each edge.
Rep rows 15–16 until piece measures approximately 6in (15cm) from cast-on edge, ending with a WS row.

Base

Row 1 (RS): K9, (ssk, k3, k2tog), k18, (ssk, k3, k2tog), k9 (46 sts).
Row 2: K1, p to last st, k1.
Row 3: K9, (ssk, k1, k2tog), k18, (ssk, k1, k2tog), k9 (42 sts).
Row 4: K1, p to last st, k1.
Row 5: K9, (k3tog), k18, (k3tog), k9 (38 sts).
Next: Break off chunky yarn, leaving a long end for sewing.
Join in waste yarn, work 4 rows in stocking stitch and then cast off.

Finishing

With darning needle and mattress stitch, sew side seams of knitted piece together; forming a tube shape. This seam will be at the centre back of the vase, so the base seam will be perpendicular to this. Use a grafting stitch to join the base seam in order to avoid a bulky ridge at the bottom; then remove the waste yarn. If the grafting stitches are uneven, use a blunt darning needle to go along and even them out. Darn in any loose ends. Finally, simply slip the vase structure into the knitted jacket and arrange as you like.

Special treasures need special containers to be kept safe. So what better place to keep your most loved secrets in than this gorgeous crocheted pot.

Tiny treasures pot

Materials

Any Aran yarn in blue (approximately 80g in
  a pure wool yarn was used for this pot)
4mm (UK8:USG/6) hook
Empty tin can and lid 3¾in (9.5cm) high ×
  4in (9.5cm) diameter
20in (50cm) length of string beading
'Safety' can opener
Darning needle and scissors

Size

The finished pot is approximately 6in (15cm) tall × 4in (10cm) diameter at highest/widest points, including lid.

Tension

Work the outer base piece for the pot: the piece should be around the same diameter as the base of the can, or just a little bigger.

Method

The pot itself (including lid) is made in crochet, amigurumi-style in spirals without joins between rounds. The outer base, outer sleeve and inner sleeve are made first. The inner base is then formed, the can popped inside the first piece and the pieces joined together to contain the can within. The lid is made in two pieces also, but a bit of stuffing is added to the top to make a 'dome' effect.

Pot

Outer base

With Aran yarn, mk floop and 1ch.
Round 1: 6dc into floop (6 sts).
Round 2: (Dc2inc) to end (12 sts).
Round 3: (1dc, dc2inc) to end (18 sts).
Round 4: (2dc, dc2inc) to end (24 sts).
Round 5: (3dc, dc2inc) to end (30 sts).
Round 6: (4dc, dc2inc) to end (36 sts).
Round 7: (5dc, dc2inc) to end (42 sts).
Round 8: (6dc, dc2inc) to end (48 sts).
Round 9: (7dc, dc2inc) to end (54 sts).
Round 10: (8dc, dc2inc) to end (60 sts) *.

Outer sleeve

Next: Work even in rounds until outer sleeve is as long as the can is high, then work 1 further round.
Do not break off yarn.

Inner sleeve

Rounds 1–2: Work even in dc.
Round 3: (8dc, dc2tog) to end (54 sts).

Next: Work even in rounds until inner sleeve is long enough to reach from the top of the can to the inner base. Work 2ss to finish, then fasten off.

Inner base

With Aran yarn, mk floop and 1ch.
Round 1: 6dc into floop (6 sts).
Round 2: (Dc2inc) to end (12 sts).
Round 3: (1dc, dc2inc) to end (18 sts).
Round 4: (2dc, dc2inc) to end (24 sts).
Round 5: (3dc, dc2inc) to end (30 sts).
Round 6: (4dc, dc2inc) to end (36 sts).
Round 7: (5dc, dc2inc) to end (42 sts).
Round 8: (6dc, dc2inc) to end (48 sts).
Round 9: (7dc, dc2inc) to end (54 sts).
Work 2ss to finish. Do not fasten off.

Join pot pieces

Place the tin can inside the inner sleeve so that the base rests on the outer base piece. Now (ss2pcs tog) so that you can join the last round of the inner sleeve to the last round of the inner base. Fasten off, secure with a knot and pull the end through to the inside of the piece to hide it away. Now tuck the inner sleeve into the inside of the pot, arranging the fabric so that it fits neatly inside and the inner base fabric rests on the inner base of the can.

Lid

Lid underside

Work as for outer base of pot to *.
Work 2ss to finish, then fasten off.

Lid top

First, wind off a small handful of the Aran yarn. This will be used for stuffing the top of the lid to create a 'dome' shape later.
Work as for outer base of pot to *.
Next: Work 2 further rounds even in dc.
Work 2ss to finish. Do not fasten off.

Join lid pieces

Place the two lid pieces tog with right sides facing outwards and lid top facing you.

Work (ss2pcs tog) halfway around, joining the two pieces together. At this point, place the can lid inside and use the small handful of yarn you wound off earlier to stuff the upper part of the lid. Cont to (ss2pcs tog) to end of round.

Fasten off and darn in end, pulling it through to the WS to hide it away.

Decoration

With darning needle and length of strung beads, decorate the lid by catching down approximately every 20th bead to create a 'spray' of beading. When you reach the end of the bead string, wrap the yarn about 15 times around where the beads meet the lid. Secure with a knot and fasten off.

Finishing

Darn in any loose ends.

Girls who have a pair of earrings for every day of the week need a special place to store them. Make this pretty pot with or without the frilly edging as a bespoke earring pot that will take pride of place on your dressing table.

Earring pot

Materials

Any DK yarn (2 strands together)
(approximately 40g in a wool/acrylic blend
    was used for this pot)
A small amount of DK 'waste' yarn
Oddments of yarn (for the earring backing pieces)
A pair of 4mm (UK8:US6) needles
A set of 4mm (UK8:US6) double-pointed needles
4mm (UK8:USG/6) hook (if working the optional frill)
Empty tin can 2in (5cm) high × 3⅓in (8.5cm) diameter
'Safety' can opener
1 sheet plastic canvas
Darning needle and scissors

Size

The pot measures approximately 2½in (6.5cm) high (including frill) × 3½in (9cm) diameter (at the base)

Tension

Approximately 5 sts and 7 rows to 1in (2.5cm) over st st using 4mm needles and two strands DK.

Pattern notes

Part-ridge pattern

Row 1 (RS): Knit.

Row 2 (WS): Purl.

Row 3: Knit.

Row 4: K9, p to end.

These four rows form the part-ridge pattern and are repeated.

Viewed from the RS, the RH 14 sts are all in stocking stitch, whereas for the LH 9 sts there is a garter stitch ridge every fourth row. The ridges make the fabric a bit shorter than stocking stitch, and so this part fits the inside of the can.

Method

The inner and outer sides are made in a single piece, knitted sideways with waste yarn at cast-on and cast-off. The outer base stitches are then picked up and knitted, decreasing for the centre. The side seam is then grafted and the waste yarn removed. The can is placed inside the cover then and double-pointed needles are used to work the inner base and close the piece. An optional frill is worked in half treble crochet. The main yarn is used double throughout except for the crocheted frill. Finally, the earring backings are made from small pieces of plastic canvas with a sewn edging.

Sides (main piece)

With 4mm needles and waste yarn, cast on 23 sts.

Work 4 rows in st st.

Break off waste yarn and join in main yarn (2 strands used together).

Rows 1–80: Work in the part-ridge pattern (20 patt reps).

Break off the 2 strands main yarn, leaving a long tail for grafting.

Join in waste yarn and work 4 rows st st.

Cast off.

Outer base

With RS of 'sides' piece facing and with 4mm needles pick up and k 42 sts along RH side of 'main' piece as folls: pick up and kfb1, pick up and k38, pick up and kfb1 (42 sts).

Row 1 (WS): Purl.

Row 2 (RS): K1, (k3, k2tog) to last st, k1 (34 sts).

Row 3: Purl.

Row 4: K1, (k2, k2tog) to last st, k1 (26 sts).

Row 5: Purl.

Row 6: K1, (k1, k2tog) to last st, k1 (18 sts).

Row 7: Purl.

Row 8: K1, (k2tog) to last st, k1 (10 sts).

Break off yarn, leaving a tail for sewing.

With darning needle thread yarn through rem sts, pull tight to close and secure with a knot.

Interim finishing

Sew the outer base seam.

Graft the side seam and remove the waste yarn.

Next, place the can inside the knitted piece so that the base of the can sits on the outer base of the fabric.

Inner base

With 4mm double-pointed needles, pick up and knit 40 sts along LH side of main piece.

Work in rounds now, with RS always facing.

Round 1: Knit.

Round 2: (K3, k2tog) to end (32 sts).

Round 3: Knit.

Round 4: (K2, k2tog) to end (24 sts).

Round 5: Knit.

Round 6: (K1, k2tog) to end (18 sts).

Round 7: Purl.

Round 8: (K2tog) to end (9 sts).

Break off yarn, leaving a tail for sewing.

With darning needle thread yarn through rem sts, pull tight to close and secure with a knot.

Finishing

With crochet hook and one strand of main yarn, work one round of half trebles all around the top – approx 2 half trebles to each row of knitting. This creates a frilly edging. Finally, darn in any loose ends and arrange frill in a wavy fashion.

Earring backings

Cut seven small rectangles in the plastic canvas, 3 'spaces' high and 7 wide. Use the contrast yarn to sew a trim around each rectangle, sewing in the ends on the back.

This pot provides a practical cash bank for little savers and proves that, in the world of crochet at least, money can grow on trees. Collect up spare pennies in the trunk of this tree and there will soon be enough for that special treat.

Money tree

Materials

Any DK yarns (approximately 100g each in brown and dark green, plus 50g in medium green were used for this pot)

A small amount of 4-ply gold lurex yarn

A 3mm (UK11:USC/2–D/3) crochet hook

A 4mm (UK8:USG/6) crochet hook

Empty tin can 5¾in (14cm) high × 2¾in (6.5cm) diameter

Recycled CD

'Safety' can opener

Darning needle and scissors

Size

Sample shown is approximately 8in (20cm) tall (including lid) × 5¾in (14cm) diameter at highest/widest points. Size may vary depending on how firmly the treetop is stuffed and the leaves arranged.

Tension

Work the outer base piece for the trunk: the piece should be around the same diameter as the base of the can, or just a little bigger.

Method

The pot is crocheted, mostly amigurumi-style, in spirals without joins between rounds. The tree trunk is made first, beginning with the outer base piece; then the inner base, inner sleeve and outer sleeve are worked in a single piece. The can is popped inside the main trunk piece and joined with slip stitch to the outer base – sealing the can inside. The treetop is made in two pieces which are stuffed and then joined with slip stitch. Leaves are worked in two shades of green and sewn on in a random fashion. Roughly half the leaves are worked from the basic leaf pattern and the remainder in freestyle variations. The base is crocheted in two pieces and joined together with a CD inside.

Trunk

Outer base

With 3mm hook and brown yarn, mk floop and 1ch.
Round 1: 6dc into floop (6 sts).
Round 2: (Dc2inc) to end (12 sts).
Round 3: (1dc, dc2inc) to end (18 sts).
Round 4: (2dc, dc2inc) to end (24 sts).
Round 5: (3dc, dc2inc) to end (30 sts).
Round 6: (4dc, dc2inc) to end (36 sts).
Round 7: (5dc, dc2inc) to end (42 sts).
Round 8: (6dc, dc2inc) to end (48 sts).
Round 9: (7dc, dc2inc) to end (54 sts).
2ss to finish, then fasten off.

Inner base

With 3mm hook and brown yarn, mk floop and 1ch.
Round 1: 6dc into floop (6 sts).
Round 2: (Dc2inc) to end (12 sts).
Round 3: (1dc, dc2inc) to end (18 sts).
Round 4: (2dc, dc2inc) to end (24 sts).
Round 5: (3dc, dc2inc) to end (30 sts).
Round 6: (4dc, dc2inc) to end (36 sts).
Round 7: (5dc, dc2inc) to end (42 sts).
Round 8: (6dc, dc2inc) to end (48 sts).

Inner sleeve

Next: Work even in dc rounds until inner sleeve is long enough to reach from base to top of the can.
Do not break off yarn, but rather continue straight on for outer sleeve.

Note: For clarity, we restart the count from 'round 1' at this point.

Outer sleeve

Round 1: (7dc, dc2inc) to end (54 sts).
Round 2: (8dc, dc2inc) to end (60 sts).
Round 3: (9dc, dc2inc) to end (66 sts).
Round 4: (10dc, dc2inc) to end (72 sts).
Rounds 5–6: Work even in dc.
Round 7: (10dc, dc2tog) to end (66 sts).
Rounds 8–9: Work even in dc.
Round 10: (9dc, dc2tog) to end (60 sts).
Rounds 11–12: Work even in dc.
Round 13: (8dc, dc2tog) to end (54 sts).
Next: Work even in dc rounds until outer sleeve is long enough to reach from top to base.
Do not fasten off.

Finishing the trunk

The main piece of the trunk (inner base, inner sleeve and outer sleeve) now looks like a long sock. Turn it inside out (so that the neater 'right side' is facing inwards). Place the inner base and sleeve into the can and arrange the fabric so that it fits neatly inside. Then roll the outer sleeve down so that it covers the outside of the can, reaching right to the bottom. Join the last round of the outer sleeve to the last round of the outer base, with one round of slip stitch. Fasten off and weave in end to finish off.

Treetop lid

First, wind off a couple of large handfuls of dark green yarn – to use for stuffing the lid later.

Lid base

With 3mm hook and dark green yarn, mk floop and 1ch.

Round 1: 6dc into floop (6 sts).
Round 2: (Dc2inc) to end (12 sts).
Round 3: (1dc, dc2inc) to end (18 sts).
Round 4: (2dc, dc2inc) to end (24 sts).
Round 5: (3dc, dc2inc) to end (30 sts).
Round 6: (4dc, dc2inc) to end (36 sts).
Round 7: (5dc, dc2inc) to end (42 sts).
Round 8: (6dc, dc2inc) to end (48 sts).
Round 9: (7dc, dc2inc) to end (54 sts).
Round 10: (8dc, dc2inc) to end (60 sts).
Round 11: (9dc, dc2inc) to end (66 sts).
Round 12: (10dc, dc2inc) to end (72 sts).
Round 13: (11dc, dc2inc) to end (78 sts).
Round 14: (12dc, dc2inc) to end (84 sts).
Round 15: (13dc, dc2inc) to end (90 sts).
Round 16: (14dc, dc2inc) to end (96 sts).
Work 2ss to finish, then fasten off.

Finishing the treetop lid

Put lid top and base together with right sides facing outwards, and (ss2pcs tog) until approximately 2in (5cm) from the end of the round. Stuff the lid unevenly with the handfuls of yarn wound off earlier, then complete the round with (ss2pcs tog) to end. Fasten off and weave in any loose ends.

Leaves

Standard leaf (make 24, 12 each in light and dark green DK)

With 4mm hook, mk 12 ch.
Row 1 (WS): Sk 1 ch (t-ch), 1ss, 2dc, 1htr, 3tr, 2htr, 2dc (11 sts).
Rotate piece right to work second row along underside of original chain.
Row 2 (WS): 2dc, 2htr, 3tr, 1htr, 2dc, 1ss (22 sts).
* Now turn piece to work from other side (this will be the RS).
Row 3 (RS): Work 11ss along the original chain (down the centre of the leaf, between rows 1 and 2).
Next: Still with RS facing, work one round of ss all around the edge of the leaf.
Fasten off *.

Freestyle leaf (make 22, 11 each in light and dark green DK)

Work in a similar fashion to the standard leaf, but vary the length of the original chain and/or the stitch sequence. For example, try this variation:
With 4mm hook, mk 11 ch.
Row 1 (WS): Sk 1 ch (t-ch), 1ss, 2dc, 1htr, 1tr, 2htr, 3dc (10 sts).
Rotate piece right to work second row along underside of original chain.
Row 2 (WS): 3dc, 3htr, 1tr, 1htr, 1dc, 1ss (20 sts).
Complete as for standard leaf from * to *.

Varying the sequence as such gives the group of leaves a more 'natural' look than if all the leaf pieces were identical.

Coins (make 8)

With 3mm hook and gold lurex yarn, mk floop and 1ch.

Round 1: 6dc into floop (6 sts).
Round 2: (Dc2inc) to end (12 sts).
Round 3: Work even in ss.

Fasten off, leaving a 6in (15cm) tail for sewing.

Base

Base underside

With 3mm hook and dark green yarn, mk floop and 1ch.

Round 1: 6dc into floop (6 sts).
Round 2: (Dc2inc) to end (12 sts).
Round 3: (1dc, dc2inc) to end (18 sts).

Round 4: (2dc, dc2inc) to end (24 sts).
Round 5: (3dc, dc2inc) to end (30 sts).
Round 6: (4dc, dc2inc) to end (36 sts).
Round 7: (5dc, dc2inc) to end (42 sts).
Round 8: (6dc, dc2inc) to end (48 sts).
Round 9: (7dc, dc2inc) to end (54 sts).
Round 10: (8dc, dc2inc) to end (60 sts).
Round 11: (9dc, dc2inc) to end (66 sts).
Round 12: (10dc, dc2inc) to end (72 sts).
Round 13: (11dc, dc2inc) to end (78 sts).
Round 14: (12dc, dc2inc) to end (84 sts).
Round 15: (13dc, dc2inc) to end (90 sts).
Round 16: (14dc, dc2inc) to end (96 sts).
Round 17: (15dc, dc2inc) to end (102 sts).
Round 18: (16dc, dc2inc) to end (108 sts).

Work 2ss to finish, then fasten off.

Base top

Work as for base underside, but do not fasten off.

Joining the base pieces

Put the two pieces together with RSs facing outwards, and (ss2pcs tog) until approx half the way around. Place the CD inside, then work the rest of the round to finish joining the pieces together. Fasten off and weave in any loose ends.

Finishing

Sew gold 'coins' onto the 'ss2pcs tog' round of the treetop lid, evenly spaced. Darn in any loose ends. Arrange leaves as you like, place lid on top of trunk and rest the tree trunk on the base.

Delightfully 'higgledy-piggledy', this beaded box provides a cheery home for little beads or other small items. Plastic canvas provides a soft and pliable structure while freestyle beading and a little loop handle adorn the lid.

Beaded box

Materials

Any DK yarn
(approximately 40g in a microfibre/acrylic blend
    yarn was used for this pot)
A pair of 4mm (UK8:US6) needles
Approximately 150 white beads
1 sheet plastic canvas
Darning needle and scissors

Size

The pot measures approximately 4in (10cm) high × 3in (7.5cm) wide/deep (excluding handle)

Tension

Approximately 5 sts and 7 rows to 1in (2.5cm) over st st using 4mm needles and a single strand of DK.

Method

The box is made first, with the outer cover knitted using two strands of yarn and creating a cross shape in stocking stitch. The inner cover uses the same pattern but with only one strand of yarn. Five little squares of plastic canvas are stitched together to form the box's structure, which sits in between the inner and outer covers. The lid echoes the box's construction method with the outer lid worked with two strands and the inner lid with just one. A square piece of plastic canvas again provides structure. Finally, beads are sewn on to decorate and a loop handle added too.

Box

Outer box cover

With 4mm needles and 2 strands of yarn, cast on 16 sts.

Note: Work in st st throughout.

Rows 1–19: Beg with a k row, work even.

Row 20 (WS): P to end, then cast on 16 sts (32 sts).

Row 21 (RS): K across the 16 new sts, the foll 16 sts and then cast on a further 16 sts (48 sts).

Row 22 (WS): P across the newest 16 sts and then p the rem 32 sts.

Rows 23–40: Work even in st st.

Row 41 (RS): Cast off 16 sts k-wise, k to end (32 sts).

Row 42 (WS): Cast off 16 sts p-wise, p to end (16 sts).

Rows 43–60: Work even in st st. Cast off k-wise.

Inner box cover

Work as for outer box cover but use just one strand of yarn throughout.

Box structure

Cut 5 pieces of plastic canvas, each approx 2½in (6.5cm) square. With darning needle and one strand of DK, sew the pieces together at the edges to form a box shape.

Putting the box together

Sew the box seams for the outer box cover as indicated in the diagram; then do the same for the inner box cover. Place the box structure in the outer box cover, then the inner box cover in the box structure so the layers are 'sandwiched' together. To join the inner and outer fabric pieces (sealing the structure within), use the tips of your knitting needles to chain-stitch all around the four sides at the top of the box. Fasten off, leaving a long tail for sewing.

Lid

Outer lid cover

With 4mm needles and 2 strands of yarn, cast on 18 sts. Beg with a k row, work 23 rows in st st. Cast off p-wise (from WS).

Inner lid cover

Work as for outer lid cover but use just one strand of yarn throughout.

Lid structure

Cut 1 piece of plastic canvas approximately 2¾in (7cm) square. With darning needle and one strand DK, use the tips of your knitting needles to chain-stitch the inner and outer lid together on 3 sides. Slip the plastic canvas square inside and then continue in needle-tip chain-stitch to close the fourth side.

Handle

With 4mm needles and one strand of DK, cast on 5 sts. Beg with a k row, work 15 rows in st st. Cast off p-wise (from WS).

Finishing

Sew the handle onto the top of the lid in a 'C' fashion.

With darning needle and one strand of yarn, string the beads. With another long length of yarn, stitch the string of beads in a freestyle fashion onto the lid.

Edgings

Use darning needle and long lengths of yarn (2 strands tog) to work satin stitch all around top edge of box and outer edge of lid.

Darn in any loose ends.

Shape box and lid by hand to suit.

Tip

Try varying the beadwork by sewing it into swirls or geometric patterns, adding lines of beads to accent the vertical lines of the box's corners or simply beading the loop handle alone.

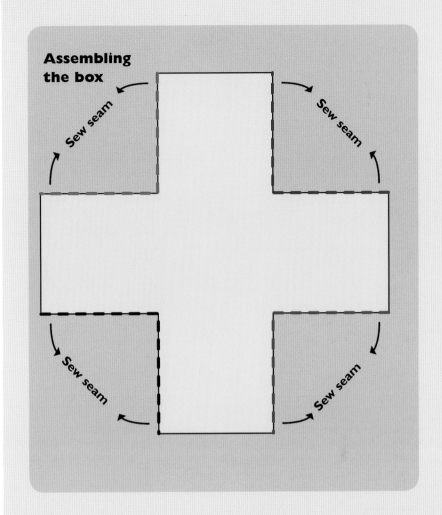

Assembling the box

Sew seam

Sew seam

Sew seam

Sew seam

Techniques

How to make precious pots to treasure

Getting started

Tension

Tension, where stated, is given as a guide only and is not critical to the success of the project.

Materials and equipment

The basic materials that you will need for most patterns are: knitting needles or crochet hook, darning needle and scissors. Additionally for some patterns you may need garden wire and pliers, plastic canvas or a container (often a recycled object) and tape.

Substituting yarn

Use what you have and save a little money! For the patterns in this book you can substitute the yarns of your liking for the ones suggested as long as the ply is roughly equivalent. Where specific yarns are mentioned this is only an indicator for the finished effect, and not a requirement.

Following patterns

Once you've decided on a pattern, it's a good idea to read it through from start to finish, and to assemble all the materials you'll need before beginning. Refer to the techniques section for guidance on any methods that are unfamiliar to you.

Knitting techniques

Casting on

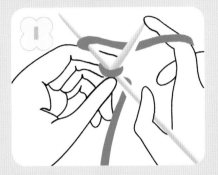

1 With a slip knot on the left-hand needle, put the right-hand needle through the loop and then pass the yarn over it.

2 Bring the yarn-over through to the front to create a new cast-on stitch.

3 Place the new stitch onto the left-hand needle.

You now have two stitches. Repeat these steps until you have the required number of stitches on the needle.

Knit (k)

1 Put the right-hand needle through the stitch on the left-hand needle (front to back), then bring the yarn over.

2 Bring the yarn-over through to the front to form a new stitch on the right-hand needle.

3 Drop the original stitch from the left-hand needle.

Purl (p)

1 Begin with the yarn to the front.

2 Put the right-hand needle through the next stitch on the left-hand needle (back to front), then draw the yarn round the needle.

3 Bring the yarn-round-needle through to the back to form a new stitch on the right-hand needle and drop the original stitch from the left-hand needle.

Casting off

1 Knit two stitches, then pass the first over the second. One stitch is 'cast off' and the other remains on the right-hand needle.

2 Knit another stitch, then pass that 'remaining' stitch over it to cast it off.

Continue in this way, knitting each stitch in turn and casting off the one before, until just one stitch remains. Break off the yarn, thread the end through that last loop and then pull tight.

A Moss stitch

Over an even number of sts:
Row 1: (Knit 1, purl 1) to end.

Over an odd number of sts:
Row 1: Knit 1, (purl 1, knit 1) to end.

Following rows: Knit over the purl stitches and purl over the knit stitches.

B Stocking stitch

Knit the 'right side' rows and purl the 'wrong side' rows.

Note: For reverse stocking stitch (rev st st), work in the opposite way i.e. purl the 'right side' rows and knit the 'wrong side' rows.

C Garter stitch

Knit every row.

D Single (1 x 1) rib

Over an even number of sts:
Row 1: (Knit 1, purl 1) to end.

Over an odd number of sts:
Row 1: Knit 1, (purl 1, knit 1) to end.

Following rows: Knit over k stitches and purl over p stitches.

E Double (2 x 2) rib

Over a multiple of 4 sts:
Row 1: (Knit 2, purl 2) to end.

Over a multiple of 4 sts plus 2:
Row 1: Knit 2, (purl 2, knit 2) to end.

Following rows: Knit over k stitches and purl over p stitches.

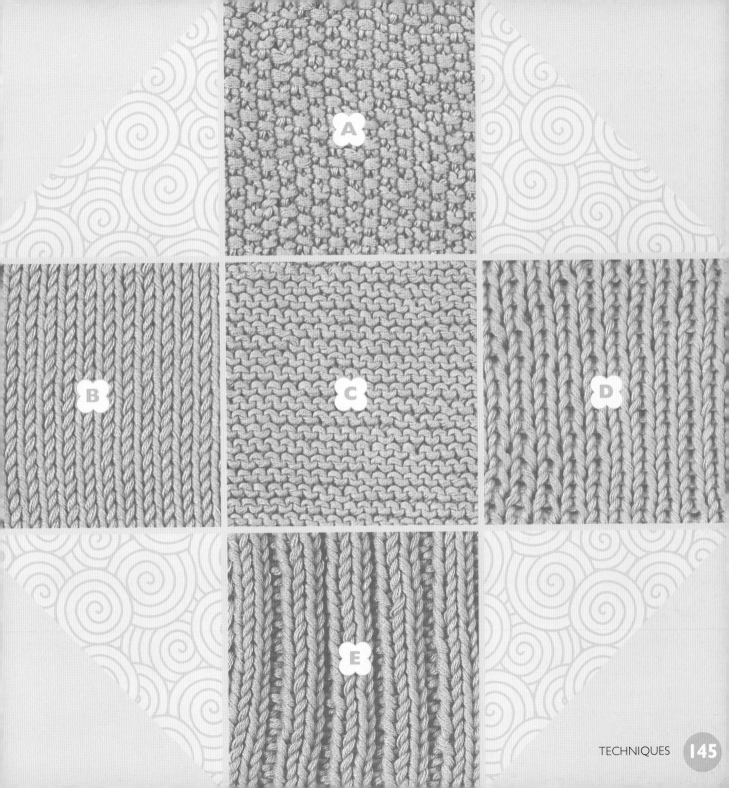

Cables

With the help of a cable needle, these decorative stitches are quite straightforward.
Stitches are slipped on to the needle and then knitted later to create the twists.

Cable 4 front (C4F)

1 Slip the next two stitches on to a cable needle and hold in front of work.

2 Knit the next two stitches from the left needle as normal, then knit the two stitches from the cable needle.

Cable 4 back (C4B)

Slip the next two stitches on to a cable needle and hold at back of work.

Knit the next two stitches from the left needle as normal, then knit the two stitches from the cable needle.

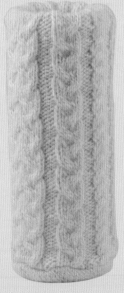

Crochet techniques

Chain stitch

This is the most basic stitch.

 Loop the yarn over the hook.

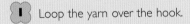 Pull the loop through to form one chain stitch.

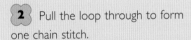 Front view of the chain.

4 Back view of the chain.

Slip stitch (ss)

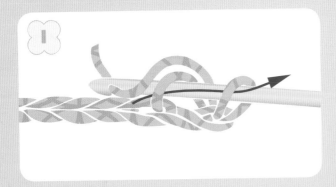 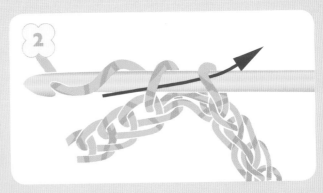

1 Hook through stitch, yarn over hook, pull through to finish off. 1 loop on hook.

2 Continue in this way for required number of slip stitches.

Double crochet (dc)

 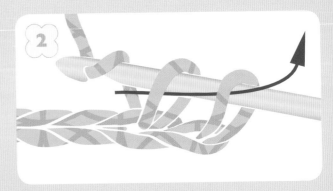

1 Hook through stitch, yarn over hook, pull through stitch. 2 loops on hook.

2 Yarn over hook, pull through both loops to finish off. 1 loop on hook.

Half treble crochet (htr)

1 Put yarn over hook, hook through stitch, yarn over hook, pull through stitch. 3 loops on hook.

2 Yarn over hook, pull through all 3 loops to finish off. 1 loop on hook.

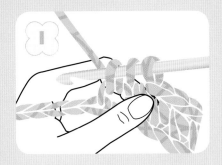

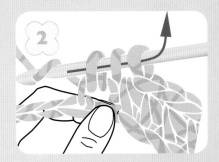

Treble crochet (tr)

1 Yarn over hook, hook through stitch.

2 Yarn over hook, pull through stitch, yarn over hook.

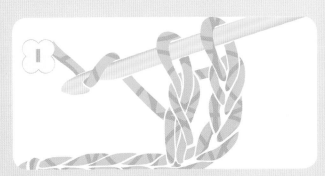

1 Pull through 2 loops. 2 loops on hook.

2 Yarn over hook, pull through 2 loops. 1 loop on hook.

Spiral rounds (circular spiral)

These are begun with a foundation loop (floop), then worked in a continuous spiral with no joining slip stitches or turning chains. The right side (RS) is always facing.

Foundation loop (floop)

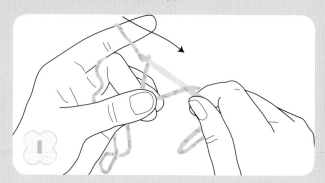

1 Yarn over hook twice, then pull through to form the loop. Do not tighten as you will be working your first round into this floop.

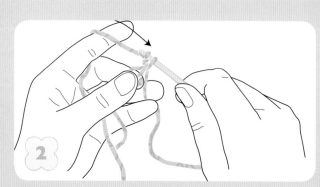

2 **Round 1:** Make 1 chain stitch (mk1ch), then work 6 double crochet stitches (6dc) into the floop. Pull the beginning end of yarn to tighten the floop. Continue straight onto the next round, without making a join or turning chain.

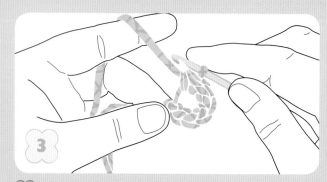

3 **Round 2:** Work a dc2inc into each st of round 1. This is a typical beginning for the pieces worked in spiral rounds.

Wired crochet

For many years I wanted to make baskets and other containers in knitting and crochet, as an alternative to the more ordinary plastic or wicker 'store-bought' pots.

I experimented with various mediums, but none really offered enough strength or structure to be particularly useful. Then I realised that heavy-duty garden wire enclosed within rounds of crochet stitches worked well to make a firm structure within the crocheted fabric, soft to the touch yet solid enough to be practical.

You will need some chunky yarn (or several strands of a finer ply used together), a crochet hook, a roll of heavy-duty garden wire and a pair of pliers. Beadwork pliers are more expensive than the hardware-store type, but really are wonderful and are best for this purpose because they have a rounded section, a flat bit and a cutting edge. However, you can make do with ordinary pliers if need be.

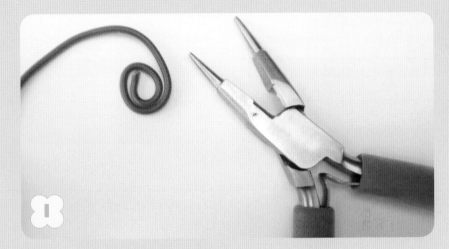

1 First make the wire floop (a double circle with wire), using the pliers to bend it into shape. The loop should be a bit bigger than the hook so that you can work your first round of stitches into it, but not so big that you end up with a big hole in the middle. A little practice is useful.

2 Work round 1 in double crochet around this ring, as you would around a yarn floop (see page 150). You can pull the wire a little to help close up the centre if necessary. Continue on in continuous spiral rounds without turns or joins, forming each crochet stitch around the wire as you go.

Tunisian crochet

Tunisian crochet (sometimes known as Afghan Stitch) results in a dense fabric with a basketweave-style surface on the right side and a very bumpy wrong side. It is often described as a mix of knitting and crochet; and the basic stitch, Tunisian simple stitch, is very quick and easy to learn.

Tunisian simple stitch (tss) is formed a little like the normal double crochet, but with some very important changes to the usual dc sequence and with a very different result.

You can buy special long hooks for Tunisian crochet, but when working fairly narrow pieces a regular crochet hook will suffice. You can use a stitch-stopper or even an eraser made to fit on the end of a pencil if you find the stitches start dropping off when all the loops are on the hook after working the first pass.

With Tunisian simple stitch, the fabric tends to curl in on itself vertically, but when the pieces are all sewn together, this won't matter.

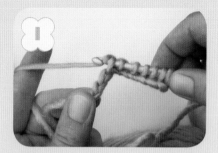

1 Make a crochet chain. On row 1 skip the first chain stitch, as if working a dc row. Work the *first half* of the dc sts in the row first, all the way across, right to left. That is: (hook through ch st, yarn over, pull up loop) to end. There will be a loop on the hook for each stitch.

3 On the second half of the row is a vertical 'bar' in front of each stitch. From row 2, when working the first pass, skip the first bar then hook through all other bars (rather than *through* the top of the stitch as for dc) and pick up each 'first half' loop through that. The second pass is always the same.

2 Change direction then make one chain stitch and work the *second half* of all the dc sts in the row all the way across, from left to right this time. So you work (yarn over, pull through 2 loops) to end. You will end up with just one loop left on the hook.

4 It takes two 'passes' to make one whole finished row and the right side is always facing you. When you are ready to complete a piece of Tunisian crochet, a tidy way to finish is to work one final pass (right to left) in slip stitch. Skip the first bar, then (through the next bar, yarn over, pull through 2 loops) to end.

Finishing touches

Mattress stitch

Place the pieces to be joined on a flat surface laid together side-by-side with right sides towards you. Using matching yarn, thread a needle back and forth with small, straight stitches. The stitches form a ladder between the two pieces of fabric, creating a nearly invisible, flat and secure seam, which is quite elastic.

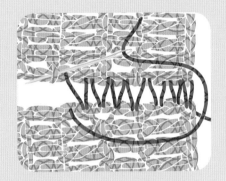

Back stitch

So called because the stitches are worked backwards, from A to B, and then the needle emerges at C for the following stitch.

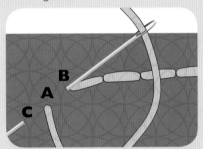

Conversions

Knitting needles

UK	Metric	US
14	2mm	0
13	2.5mm	1
12	2.75mm	2
11	3mm	–
10	3.25mm	3
–	3.5mm	4
9	3.75mm	5
8	4mm	6
7	4.5mm	7
6	5mm	8
5	5.5mm	9
4	6mm	10
3	6.5mm	10.5
2	7mm	10.5
1	7.5mm	11
0	8mm	11
00	9mm	13
000	10mm	15

Crochet hooks

UK	Metric	US
14	2mm	B/1
13	2.25mm	–
12	2.5mm	C/2
11	3mm	–
10	3.25mm	D/3
9	3.5mm	E/4
8	4mm	G/6
7	4.5mm	7
6	5mm	H/8
5	5.5mm	I/9
4	6mm	J/10
3	6.5mm	K/10.5
2	7mm	–
0	8mm	L/11
00	9mm	M–N/13
000	10mm	N–P/15

Abbreviations

approx	approximately
beg	begin(ning)
ch	chain stitch
cm	centimetre(s)
cont	continue
dc	double crochet
dc2inc	double crochet twice in next stitch (to increase)
dc2tog	double crochet two stitches together (to decrease)
dec	decrease
DK	double knitting
Floop	foundation loop
foll	following
htr	half treble/half treble stitch
inc	increase by working twice into the stitch
K/k	knit
kfb	knit into front and back of stitch
k-wise	knitwise, as if to knit
k2tog	knit 2 sts together
k3tog	knit 3 sts together
LH	left-hand side
mk	make
m1	make 1 stitch
P/p	purl
patt	pattern
p2tog	purl 2 sts together
p3tog	purl 3 sts together
p-wise	purlwise, as if to purl
rem	remaining

rep	repeat	ss2pcs tog	slip stitch 2 pieces together	tr	treble crochet stitch or treble
rev st st	reverse stocking stitch	ss	slip stitch	tr2tog	treble crochet 2 stitches together (to decrease)
RH	right-hand side	ssk	slip 1 st (k-wise), slip another st in the same way, then knit them both together	tss	Tunisian simple stitch
rnd	round			wk	work
RS	right side of work	st(s)	stitch(es)	WS	wrong side of work
sk	skip	st st	stocking stitch	yd	yard (s)
sl	slip	tbl	through back loop(s)	*	work instructions following *, then repeat as directed
sl-knot	slip knot	t-ch	turning chain		
spiral	working in continuous rounds without joins	tog	together	( )	repeat instructions inside brackets as directed

About the author

Gina Alton learned the basics of knitting and crochet at the age of five, with help from her grandma Mildred and neighbour Ann. From this humble beginning grew a lifelong passion for all things yarny. Now grown up (more or less), her career is divided between working for *Knitting* magazine, editing patterns, creating technical drawings and teaching crafts as well as designing pots, toys, home furnishings and games – all centred on the beloved arts of knitting and crochet. She lives in the beautiful heart of Devon, England with her children Allie and Fred. Her children, with their boundless energy and contagious enthusiasm, are great sources of inspiration for new designs.

Gina wrote her first book, *Crocheted Finger Puppets*, while fighting cancer and the second, *Pots to Knit and Crochet*, while recovering from the battle. This book is dedicated to Marla Cilley (a.k.a. the FlyLady), for teaching that anything is possible in babysteps.

Creating beautiful and useful things with simply a length of yarn plus needles or a hook – with a dash of imagination and a splash of inspiration, right from the heart – is wonderfully therapeutic and rewarding. If you have any queries, comments or suggestions regarding these patterns, Gina can be contacted at www.CraftTherapy.biz.

Index

To place an order, or to request a catalogue, contact:
GMC Publications Ltd
Castle Place, 166 High Street, Lewes, East Sussex,
BN7 1XU, United Kingdom
Tel: +44 (0)1273 488005   **Fax:** +44 (0)1273 402866
www.gmcbooks.com